DRAW
CLOSE
TO THE
FIRE

Other Books by Terry Wardle

*The Transforming Path: A Christ-centered Approach to
Spiritual Formation*
*Healing Care, Healing Prayer: Helping the Broken Find
Wholeness in Christ*
*Wounded: How You Can Find Inner Wholeness and
Healing in Him*
One to One: A Practical Guide to Friendship Evangelism
Exalt Him: Designing Dynamic Worship Services
Whispers of Love in Seasons of Fear
The Soul's Journey to God's Embrace

DRAW CLOSE TO THE FIRE

Finding God in the Darkness

TERRY WARDLE

LEAFWOOD
P U B L I S H E R S
an imprint of Abilene Christian University Press

DRAW CLOSE TO THE FIRE

PUBLISHERS
an imprint of Abilene Christian University Press

Copyright 1998, 2004 by Terry Wardle

ISBN 0-9728425-8-6

Printed in the United States of America

Leafwood Publishers is an imprint of
Abilene Christian University Press.

1648 Campus Court
Abilene, Texas 79601
1-877-816-4455 toll free

For current information about all Leafwood titles, visit our website:
www.leafwoodpublishers.com

Dedication

To all those who are desperate

for God's Healing Presence

Contents

Introduction

I f you have followed the way of Jesus for very long, you know well that this pilgrimage is a journey of peaks as well as valleys. There are incredibly beautiful and refreshing places along the path of faith, and times that you cross treacherous, even frightening terrain. There are days when the brightness of God's presence offers joy and peace. And sometimes the darkness of night closes in, bringing with it that debilitating discomfort that threatens to undo you.

The question I ask is this: How do you respond when you find yourself in that dark, lonely and often frightening place? If you are like most of us, you experience a very real drive either to turn back or to pray that the darkness will pass as quickly as possible. This reaction is natural and understandable. Part of my own Christian pilgrimage involved an indescribably dark season. I wanted one thing and one thing only: out of there! But any reaction to avoid the dark times and places God brings your way is the wrong response by far.

As upsetting and unsettling as painful times are, you must learn to be patient and watchful as you move through them. Why? Because there are priceless treasures to be gained even in the dark times. God has placed blessings in the seasons of suffering and trial that are capable of changing your life, enhancing your intimacy with Him and increasing your spiritual vitality and personal growth. The question is, how do you lay hold of these treasures found only in the darkness of difficulty and discomfort?

You must draw close to the fire of God's presence, where His light brings them into full view.

When early pioneers set off into the frontier, they hoped to journey into a rich and fertile land. But they had no illusions about the pilgrimage they were undertaking. It would be difficult and dangerous, particularly as the blackness of night fell. In response to the darkness, they would build a large bonfire in the center of the camp. It served to illumine the area so they could clearly see any potential threat from man or animal. It also provided warmth against the chilling cold that came with the setting of the sun. People found it safest and most comforting as they drew close to the light and warmth of the fire.

This book is about twelve principles of life that can help you in the darkness to draw close to the fire and find God. Each principle will serve as a tool to help you locate, unearth and refine all the hidden blessings God offers you through difficulty and trial. Each is based on a spiritual precept found in His Word. They were important to me on my own journey through the dark night, and have since helped many fellow pilgrims passing through their own places of pain and suffering. They also serve as foundational principles of personal renewal and restoration at the Institute of Formational Counseling of Ashland Theological Seminary in Ashland, Ohio. I pray that you will embrace these truths as you make your own pilgrimage through the dark valley. At the end of each chapter I have placed a short reading list. These books further develop the principle being discussed, tooling you all the more to find God's hidden blessings along the way.

Thanks to Leonard Allen of Leafwood Publishers for publishing this book. And thanks to those who allowed me to share their stories—an invaluable contribution to the book. Many of the names found in these pages are fictitious in order to protect these special people, but the stories themselves are all true.

Terry Wardle
Ashland, Ohio

God Is within the Darkness

his chapter should be affixed with a warning label, particularly for those in some degree of emotional or spiritual conflict. *Reading it will not initiate a feel-good experience that quickly calms the high seas of internal upheaval.* In fact, it may even unsettle you, causing you to set this book aside.

Please don't. I know the turmoil of suffering and the desperate drive for relief, and I believe this material will help the broken. But it is no quick fix. Instead, as you read, you will be challenged to find something even greater than feeling better or solving your problem. I want you to see that God is in the darkness, waiting to meet you with incredible love, compassion and intimacy. There may be short-term pain, but read on, for in the end there is peace—lasting peace.

"Get Me Out of Here!"

The most important and transforming journey of my life was not one of my own choosing. It began in the spring of 1992 as I was nearing the end of my second decade of vocational Christian ministry. As was typical of my approach to Christian service, I was trying to manage an extremely demanding schedule. It was the result of a very unhealthy philosophy I had adopted, believing it was far better to burn out than rust out for the Lord. In May of that year I was teaching full-time at Simpson Graduate School, serving as senior pastor of a congregation numbering more than eight hundred, revising a previously published work and preparing for an intensive week of lecturing at Alliance Theological Seminary. In addition, I had my normal responsibilities as a husband and father of three. This fast-paced work ethic had always been my style and it had contributed to my quick ascent to positions of responsibility as a pastor, administrator and educator. I was soon to discover that it was also leading me along the path to physical and emotional upheaval.

For some time I had been experiencing growing levels of anxiety and unusual periods of fear. I simply ignored what my body was trying to tell me, however, as well as warnings from my wife and closest friends. I pushed on, working all the harder to compensate for the discomfort. But by the end of spring I was on the ragged edge, beginning the journey into almost total breakdown. What followed was a season of debilitating panic attacks. Without warning I would grow light-headed, find my heart racing and experience an uncontrollable urge to run in fear. The feelings were irrational, but no amount of self-talk worked to stop them. It happened at church while I was preaching, in stores, at home, while I was driving the car, almost everywhere. At their worst, panic attacks occurred ten to fifteen times a day. Eventually they led to my being homebound. I began to avoid any place or person that triggered these frightening and exhausting adrenaline rushes.

Following this I fell into deep depression, marked by persistent crying, isolation in a darkened bedroom and feelings of dread and black despair. At times I felt hopeless, assaulted with uncontrollable thoughts of a godless eternal night. For weeks I was unable to read and I found Scripture condemning or irrelevant. This only heightened my levels of anxiety, fear, panic and depression. The cycle was set to breed on itself. It eventually led to counseling, hospital treatment and several months away from work.

Had I anticipated this pain-filled pilgrimage, I would have done anything to avoid it. Anything! More than a few times I tried to stop and turn back, to no avail. I was often angry and resentful that this unwelcome journey was seemingly forced on me. I was in deep emotional turmoil, fearing for my very sanity and sure that my ministry, reputation and future were ruined permanently. From my perspective, absolutely nothing positive or good could ever result from all this heartache and chaos. As far as I was concerned, it was all evil, unloving, unfair and totally unnecessary.[1]

Avoid Pain at Any Price

My reaction to this season of suffering came quite naturally, taught by a society convinced that pain and brokenness are to be avoided at all cost. Kitty Muggeridge, in her introduction to a recent edition of Jean-Pierre de Caussade's classic work, *The Sacrament of the Present Moment,* ably defines our culture as

> abandoned to the fantasies and arrogance of the pursuit of happiness which so quickly becomes a pursuit of pleasure; in which suffering, mental or physical, must be drugged out of existence, in which there is no place for the Cross of Christianity.[2]

In this context I learned that it is the whole, the healthy, the rich and the famous who are to be envied and modeled. The sick, particularly those in emotional upheaval, are set apart or at best spoken of in hushed terms. Such people are seen as weak, undependable and repulsively needy.

My experience in the local church was not all that different. After years of education in the principles of leadership and watching the value system of many in the organized church, my perception was that "blessed are the successful, the bright, the powerful, the together." So, for nearly two decades of ministry, I had given my all to be among the blessed. This point of view was reinforced when one influential colleague, on hearing of my breakdown, told me to "keep it all quiet or it will ruin your ministry."

My attitude and the general atmosphere regarding brokenness affected the way I responded to my forced march into the valley of sorrow. At first all I wanted was out! I was gripped with fear, confused and stuck in a lifeless bog. I felt as though I had unknowingly crossed that thin line between sanity and insanity. I cried until I thought I could not shed another tear, only to learn there was an ocean of sorrow still there. When anyone asked how they could help, my answer was always the same: "Get me out of here!"

It did not take long for me to realize I was not going to stop this journey, so my focus changed. Since I could not get out, maybe I could do something to deaden the pain. Surely that was a proper goal. After all, we spend most of our lives trying to avoid or anesthetize pain. I was like a child wanting to fall asleep in the back seat of the car during the long drive to Grandma's house. I wanted to doze through the whole thing, waking when I reached the final destination.

It is possible to find people uncaring enough to medicate any and all pain out of existence. I have met many fellow pilgrims who found caregivers willing to serve this unhealthy goal. My friends may now feel no pain, but they are also numb to the real purposes of suffering and losing more than they could ever realize. Thankfully I was led to professionals who believe that medication should not mask pain, but stabilize a person enough to face it and the underlying wounds that need healing.

Embracing the Journey

Healing finally began for me when, after much struggle and failure, I set aside my selfish and childish goals and, by grace, found a new way to face this pain-filled pilgrimage. The shift in focus revolutionized my life, my relationships and my ministry. It brought me into intimacy with God, a new love for my wife and family, a new compassion for the broken and a new ministry to Christian leaders. It initiated changes that, by the power of the Holy Spirit, continue to this very day.

Instead of begging to get out, or trying desperately to silence the pain, I learned that people in crisis must embrace the journey, as difficult as that is. Rather than expend energy avoiding all suffering as evil, of little good, unloving or unfair, we must let the pain-filled path drive us to the God who is good in all He does. We will soon discover that in His hands, the object of deepest sorrow can become the source of our greatest blessing.

This approach will not quickly alleviate the trial, nor will it answer all the questions suffering brings. But I know that God waits to be found in the midst of the darkness, so we must learn to embrace it. There God will cause us to see things we would never find in the light—truths, experiences of His love and faithfulness, and new understanding about ourselves and the broken world in which we live.

I have just looked out my second-story window, near the desk where I am writing. Jeff and Beth Spencer have pulled into our driveway. They are here to find help and direction during an excruciatingly painful time in their lives. Just six weeks ago their infant daughter, McKenzie Rose, died.

Beth and Jeff had tried to have a child for more than five years. They prayed diligently that the Lord would allow them to be parents, and we all rejoiced when the news came that Beth was pregnant. At birth they discovered that their newborn daughter had Down syndrome and would require very special care. Undaunted, Jeff and Beth embraced this child with love and delight. They saw her through heart surgery and arduous months of recuperation. All this time joy radiated from them because of their little McKenzie Rose. But long after recovering fully from surgery, she fell ill with pneumonia and all too suddenly was gone.

Since that devastating loss, Beth and Jeff have come to our house at least twice a week. They are struggling to hold on along a dark journey not of their own choosing. They are reaching out for support, not sure they can find their way on their own.

If by God's grace I can help them embrace this awful pain—instead of running, lashing out or denying it—I believe it will transform their lives. God is in the darkness, weeping with them, longing to love, comfort and heal their deep wound. Their only hope for wholeness, as harsh as it sounds, lies within their suffering, for there they will find God ready to pour out His love and strength. Because I love them, I must encourage them continually into this "cloud of unknowing."[3] Dear Lord, help us all.

Maybe you are on such a journey, caught in painful circumstances that seem unbearable. Your insides may hurt so much that you fear falling apart. It could be a health issue, relationship, lost dream, spiritual upheaval or even death. Maybe you are caught in an unrelenting addiction.

Fear may have such a grip that you think you are trapped forever. I know these feelings, for I too traversed that desperate path. Know this: *How you respond to this dark hour is critical!* Don't run or beg for sleep or lash out or betray your Lord. Embrace the pain and find God in the darkness. It is there that He waits to bless you.[4]

"Surely God Is in This Place"

Even a casual reading of Scripture reveals that God waits to meet His people in the midst of darkness. At times it is a harsh valley brought on by sinful choices—the ugly consequence of rebellion. Sometimes the onslaught of evil against good people results in a season of painful night they did not seek or deserve. But whatever the cause, there is always a Kingdom purpose, realized when people seek God within the storm.

Most amazing are the repeated references indicating that God often designs the dark night sovereignly.[5] We find in Scripture that He is not a distant, passive observer, but is intricately present for purposes of refining and reorienting those He loves. Consider the following texts, a mere sampling of many in Scripture teaching us that God is in the valley of suffering.

In Psalm 119 the writer confesses that affliction actually put him back on course. Rather than curse God for allowing the pain, he blesses Him, declaring that "you are good, and what you do is good" (verse 68). In verse 75 he says, "In faithfulness you have afflicted me." Imagine that! The psalmist sees God as the cause of his suffering; but rather than lash out, he praises Him! Why? Because he embraces the trial and seeks God in the darkness. Upon finding God, he receives joy and peace that make the suffering pale in comparison.

This same experience awaits us all.

The book of Isaiah concerns, in part, the judgment of God on Israel and her impending exile into Babylon. Her rebellion and sin caused God to raise up a foreign people as His instruments of wrath. While the bondage promised to be severe, however, God assured His people of redemption and His faithfulness. Speaking through Isaiah, the Lord declared:

> "When you pass through the waters, I will be with you; and when you pass through the rivers, they will not sweep over you. When you walk through the fire, you will not be burned."
>
> Isaiah 43:2

Where was God during Israel's journey through bondage, pain and sorrow? Right in the midst of the darkness. We must see this for our own journeys, gaining strength to embrace the storm and flood and fire as the very places to find God.

I have found Psalm 66 particularly helpful, guiding my own response to the emotional upheaval brought on by rejection. The writer sees God's hand at the center of seasons of affliction. He calls God's people to bless the Lord for taking them through trial, believing it prepares them for the future. I particularly appreciate Eugene Peterson's paraphrase of verses 8–12 from *The Message:*

> Bless our God, oh peoples!
> Give him a thunderous welcome!
> Didn't he set us on the road to life?
> Didn't he keep us out of the ditch?
> He trained us first,
> passed us like silver through refining fires,
> Brought us into hardscrabble country,
> pushed us to our very limit,
> Road-tested us inside and out,

took us to hell and back.
Finally he brought us to this well-watered place.

The psalmist is talking about tough, painful times of darkness, bondage and oppression. Yet he does not lash out in anger, but instead praises God. Why? Because the events drove the people to the Lord, where they discovered His love, faithfulness and compassion. The psalmist clearly believes that discovering those aspects of God far outweighs the suffering, pain and brokenness that preceded.

Nowhere is this principle more obvious than in the life and teachings of Jesus and His followers. Brokenness and suffering were a given, not only as a result of combating evil, but also as necessary conditions to truly experiencing God. Just consider the Sermon on the Mount. Talk about an upside-down Kingdom! Jesus tells us it is the broken who are blessed, the unfortunate who are the most blessed of all. Words like *poor, mourning, meekness, hunger* and *thirst* are usually associated with great loss. Yet Jesus blesses these conditions in the hearts and lives of people. Why? Because they can be the pathway to Kingdom life and spiritual abundance!

Jesus came for the lost, associated with the dirty, spent time with losers and died for sinners. He told His followers to look for Him in the midst of hunger, thirst, poverty and oppression (see Matthew 25:34–40). It was there He spent His life setting men and women free for intimacy with God. Even in His death, our Lord associated with the despised, rejected and condemned. What is the point? Don't look to find Jesus only in health and wholeness, holiness and happiness. He is in the midst of pain and suffering, ready to draw the willing into the deeper things of His Kingdom.

Paul's teaching resonates with this theme. He tells believers that suffering has a purpose, that we should rejoice in the valley (see Romans 5:1–5). While it sounds preposterous, he assures Christians that it is part of the maturing process. In 2 Corinthians Paul thanks the Lord for the gracious favor that enabled him to experience great hardship and despair. It happened, he said, in order to break any self-reliance and cause him to trust God more (see 2 Corinthians 1:8–11).

What a perspective! God can be found in the valley.

These are but a few of countless Scriptures that teach Christians to embrace pain and allow it to draw them to God. James, Peter and the writer of Hebrews lift up this principle equally.[6] The Lord wants us to learn from trials, not run from them. He desires that we find Him in the midst of them rather than concentrate solely on getting out. In an age addicted to comfort, Christians need to take another look at God's Word with reference to suffering. It speaks volumes to the broken, giving incredible reason to hold on and trust God in the midst of pain.

Sacrament of the Present Moment

I must tell you that my initial reaction to this principle was not positive. It was easier believing that my dark period was evil or an illness and that God would get me out. Realizing that He was actually involved made me angry. I had been experiencing deep emotional pain for too long! What started as days led to months of deep struggle and a few years of ongoing battle.

The impact of my illness on my wife was initially very unsettling. Her confidence in my contribution to the security of our future became tenuous at best. As for our teenage children, the dark night caused them confusion and concern. In addition to the emotional price, hospitalization and therapy took all our savings and more.

To discover that God was in this darkness did not please me. And frankly, I let Him know my feelings in no uncertain terms. You may be at that place right now, and if so, I understand. More important, God understands!

Yet an amazing transformation began to take place. As I wrestled with God in the darkness, I began to know Him better and better. His love, patience and faithfulness slowly became present realities as never before. He caused me to see in the dark what I had failed to perceive in the light. It still hurt, but somehow, now that God was there, peace began to settle into my spirit. Cleansing, release and growth were taking place. My wife, Cheryl, and our children also began to see that the pain of these days opened the way to an entirely new and exciting walk with the Lord. Their trust in the Lord grew stronger and they experienced a compassion for the broken as never before. Slowly I saw that He *was* good and there was a purpose to all this.

Even now, after several years, the journey is not without pain. Like Jacob after wrestling with God, I have been left with a limp. Seasons of anxiety threaten at times, and I have lingering avoidance issues yet to conquer. But I have learned to seek God immediately, thankful that now the handicap draws me closer to Him and brings with it a healthy humility regarding life. While my ministry to the broken is a sacred trust, this infirmity reminds me that His strength is made perfect in weakness. Thus my weakness really is a precious gift.

This concept was developed by the Christian mystics of the fifteenth to eighteenth centuries. Their insights helped me better understand the severe mercy God often brings to His servants. Author after author reinforced the notion that God is in everything that comes at us in every moment. This makes each moment a sacred opportunity to experience our Lord, if we seek Him there by faith.

Jean-Pierre de Caussade, a spiritual director of the late seventeenth century, wrote:

> Perfection comes . . . not through reason, enlightenment or reflection, but through every affliction sent by God. . . . It is in these afflictions, which succeed one another each moment, that God, veiled and obscured, reveals Himself, mysteriously bestowing His grace in a manner quite unrecognized by souls who feel only weakness in bearing their cross. . . .[7]

Such a radical perspective on suffering revolutionizes one's approach to what sixteenth-century Spanish monk St. John of the Cross called "the dark night of the soul." Instead of seeking counselors committed to getting us out, we need spiritual directors able to help us discover God in the midst, allowing Him to complete the work that sent us there in the first place.

François Fénelon, the seventeenth-century French bishop, instructed his disciples to embrace whatever God brought into their lives:

> God does not transform you on a bed of light, life and grace. His transformation is done on the cross in darkness, poverty and death. See God's hand in the circumstances of your life. Do you want to experience true happiness? Submit yourself peacefully and simply to God and bear your sufferings without struggle.[8]

Few in the church, at least in the United States, incorporate this principle in their approach to recovery. Yet it resonates with Scripture and calls us to surrender to the sovereignty of God in our lives. Dr. Larry Crabb profoundly exposes the importance of this stance toward suffering in his book *Finding God*. For those unaccustomed to or uncomfortable with the Christian mystics, Crabb's work is a first-rate alternative. You will most likely find his writing disturbing yet life-changing in its implications to the broken. Dr. Crabb, critical of many popular approaches to counseling, encourages people to find God in the storm. "People who value resolution of pain over learning to love," he writes, "often jump onto the counseling bandwagon that offers solutions to problems rather than a pathway to God."[9] To his mind—and I agree—solving problems is a poor substitute to finding God in the midst of difficulty.

Many Christians are familiar with *The Practice of the Presence of God* by Brother Lawrence. This short work is a classic appreciated for its simple, clear presentation of life-changing truth. Here, too, we read that the journey into darkness is far more blessing than curse for the man or woman hungry to find God:

> The men of the world do not comprehend these truths, nor is it to be wondered at. . . . They consider sickness as a pain to nature and not as a favor from God; and seeing it only in that light, they find nothing but grief and distress. But those who consider sickness as coming from the hand of God, as the effect of His mercy, such commonly find in it great sweetness and consolation.[10]

I am not advocating that we never seek healing or help. I pray for the sick regularly and go to the doctor when necessary. But there are more important goals than health and happiness. Often God meets us in pain and suffering to accomplish far greater purposes in our lives. We must learn to surrender to that work when it is upon us and allow God to transform us.

Why Is This Happening to Me?

God has not obligated Himself to answer every question at our demand. There are no answers at times except the cross for why we go through what we do. Several key issues, however, are often the focus of a person's dark night. While each can be developed in detail, I will present them only briefly to stimulate personal insight and consideration.

Intimacy First and Foremost

Nothing is more important to your life than developing intimacy with God and communing with Him. It is so important that, in comparison, anything else you invest in is a distant second.

Christianity is fundamentally a love relationship with God, available through faith in Christ and nurtured through the faithful embrace of a variety of spiritual disciplines. The Holy Spirit will empower your participation in such activities as prayer, Scripture reading, solitude, silence and service. The purpose of this empowerment is relational, drawing you toward spiritual union with God and maturity for character and service. Compromise this and you put at risk the vitality and effectiveness of your Christian experience.

Most Christian leaders agree with this priority in theory. But practically, what we know best is how to work for God, not how to commune with Him. Christian service has for countless believers become the substitute for intimacy with the Lord; and the implications are far-reaching, including burnout, broken families, workaholism, emotional upheaval and rampant ineffectiveness.

For several years I have had the opportunity to teach a graduate course for Christian leaders in spiritual formation. Each story is virtually identical—of ministry demands that squeeze out the very disciplines that give life and relationship with Christ. Leaders are overinformed in the "doing" of ministry and grossly impoverished in the spirit.

My own experience was tragically similar until the Lord brought on the dark night. It was what Eugene Peterson refers to in his book *Under the Unpredictable Plant,* as a season of *askesis*—an involuntary confinement forcing one to listen to the voice of God. I believe He whispered to me for years but I did not listen. My own issues and the models of ministry I embraced were noisy, drowning out the voice of God. And so, out of incredible love, He chose to shout through the pain of depression and anxiety. Even then I did not perceive the issue at first. But over time I heard His voice, calling me into the stillness and rest of intimacy, and by His grace my life has been transformed.

Change in our relationship with God could come by an easier way, but all too often we are blinded by our own stubbornness. In the darkness, however, we see clearly that inebriation with Him is life's greatest treasure—one worth selling all for, even when the price includes suffering. Could it be that God is waiting in your own dark night for this very same purpose? Has He been longing to draw you into incredible union, but you ignored His whispers of love? Is this season of pain God's megaphone, calling loudly for your attention and surrender? You will know only as you press in and find Him there.

Who Is in Control Here, Anyway?

It does not take long, following your entrance into this world, to realize that this is not a safe place. You arrive vulnerable and glutted with needs. Then, over time, you develop a sophisticated system designed to control your environment. You incorporate emotional responses, behaviors and relational preferences, all serving your need to be safe and secure. Some of your actions are aggressive, others manipulative, still others selectively passive. Underneath it all is anxiety that energizes your choices. Over time, as you wear yourself out "managing" your world, emotional upheaval begins to rip at your life.

Frankly, far too many people become Christians because they think God will fit nicely into their system of control. After all, isn't He there to heal, provide, protect, rescue and help when needed? While God may tolerate such a basis of relationship in immaturity, sooner or later you will be challenged to stop using Him and meet Him for who He truly is.

Cathy Zeimer is in a painful place right now, struggling to let go of her misconceptions about God. She is a young missionary who, before becoming a Christian, struggled with a very manipulative personality. Her behavior was rooted in significant insecurity and emptiness as a result of an abusive home life. On finding Christ, Cathy came alive with new joy. Much about her changed, particularly how she used other people to her own ends. Prayer became a way of life as she gave endless hours to intercession. She saw countless places where God intervened in response to her prayers. Lifting petitions to the Lord was her delight.

That is, until Teri. Teri was a young girl Cathy had befriended who died after a brief illness. Ever since, Cathy has been in a dark night. Her anger and disappointment with God are both deep and wide. It was easy for me to see, talking with her, that she had believed God answered prayer, always and abundantly. To her it was part of the "contract benefits" of being a Christian. Granted, it might take time, fervency and faith, but she believed He would come through. Until now!

While Cathy is in deep pain, it is a blessing and God is right in the midst of the darkness, breaking her of a spirit of control. Intercession had really just become her new "Christian" coping mechanism. She was not praying so as to participate in God's activity. Cathy was praying to get God to do *her* will, not His. In fact, instead of "working" people, she was trying to "work" God.

God will allow night to set in, if necessary, to strip His people of their control, so they can rest in His control. His control does not mean we will never face trial, heartache, difficulty or disappointment. Resting in His control means trusting that whatever happens will ultimately fit perfectly into His eternal, love-based plan for our lives.

While surrendering to His Lordship does not necessarily mean you will be "safe," it does promise security in Him. This security brings you that peace that passes understanding, linked to the belief that God's presence and purpose are constant regardless of the circumstance. Experiencing this peace often demands a painful season of stripping, letting go of control in order to find Him. God will use pain, as He is doing in Cathy's life, to draw you to true faith and trust in His sufficiency. God does not want you to embrace Him only because He will meet your needs. He wants you to seek Him in order to know, enjoy and trust His love-filled presence. If necessary, He will use darkness to shed this light in your heart.

Conformed to the Image of Christ

Garrett Jensen was sitting in my office when I arrived. As our eyes met, I could see that his heart was heavy and that he had been crying. Garrett was struggling through one of the most difficult years of his life. It had been only ten months since he had turned back to the Lord after years of wandering. Garrett had been pressing in faithfully to grow in Christ, despite some devastating circumstances since making this commitment.

Soon after Garrett's decision to return to the Lord, his wife of eleven years left him for another man. The tragic result of this included an ongoing custody battle for his two sons. The emotional turmoil, including deep loneliness and feelings of abandonment, was taking its toll. Garrett had come to my office that day so we could pray together, but now he began to cry.

"Why is this happening, Terry?" he exclaimed. "Where is God in all this? I can't take any more."

For a long time I said nothing, choosing simply to sit there with my arm on his shoulder and weep with him.

After a while I sensed the Holy Spirit quicken me. All I said was, "Garrett, you are looking more and more like Jesus all the time."

With this he began to weep uncontrollably and fell to the floor.

No more was said, but the Spirit was helping him see that regardless of the cause, God was using this darkness to transform his life.

That day proved a turning point for Garrett Jensen. The promise of Romans 8:28–29 came alive to him:

> We know that in all things God works for the good of those who love him, who have been called according to his purpose. For those God foreknew he also predestined to be conformed to the likeness of his Son.

I am sure you know Romans 8:28. But I believe verse 29 must accompany it in your understanding. God, by His love and grace, will use all things for the purpose of conforming His children into the likeness of Jesus. Our Father works through the "all things" of trial, suffering and loss to shape in us the character and holiness of our beautiful Lord.

This conforming goes on throughout our lives and includes those seasons of darkness that purge self and sin from our nature. The Father works, within the context of suffering, to reshape us to the very core of our beings. He lays hold of us in such times, shaking us loose from our sinfully self-centered way of getting what we want. Our Father does this so that the new, love-based nature of Christ can flourish within.

Madame Jeanne Guyon wrote of this in her letter to Fénelon. He was going through a difficult time and she offered him the following insights:

> God wants to lead you, and all He needs from you is your permission to let Him. In order for this to happen, you must allow yourself to die daily, moment by moment.
>
> This is the way of pure faith: to lose your will in God's. This will leave you with nothing to hold on to but God, and this is not easily accomplished.
>
> As you reach this state of death, which comes after an experience of complete poverty and misery, you will discover great truths. These truths are known only by those who are taught by God.[11]

Once again the principle is before you: Our Father can be found in the darkness, but to find Him there you must yield. This does not mean you should fail to express your heartache, loss and confusion along the journey through the dark night. You need to be honest about your feelings, grieve your losses and ask your questions. The season is far from easy, and it does no good pretending otherwise. It is a time of weakness and desperation.

But learn to surrender your wants in this time to the heavenly Father, resting them all in His loving hands. By faith you can embrace Him in the midst of pain and suffering, yielding to God's greater work that brings intimacy, freedom and the selfless character of Christ Jesus within. There is something more important than finding a way out! If you desire, you can find God.

May I quote a portion of Scripture that became an important signpost on my own journey? It speaks of hope and purpose in suffering, and I lay my claim repeatedly to this promise:

> I will give you the treasures of darkness, riches stored in secret places, so that you may know that I am the LORD, the God of Israel, who summons you by name.
>
> Isaiah 45:3

Are you interested in uncovering the treasures hidden in secret places along your own path of difficulty and trial? Do you long to find warmth and light from the fire of God's presence in the midst of your own dark night? If the answer is yes, then read on. The following chapters deal with biblical principles that will help you find the spiritual riches God has placed there just for you. The principles will serve as a miner's tools, enabling you to locate and uncover priceless truths hidden in the dark and difficult places along life's pathway. Be assured, if you not only read what is said but apply the principles to your life, the treasures of God in secret places will be yours. And there is not a more precious treasure than the one we will now discuss—developing an ever-growing relationship with the glorious Lord Christ.

For Further Reading

Finding God by Larry Crabb
The Storm Within by Mark Littleton
Under the Unpredictable Plant by Eugene Peterson
The Practice of the Presence of God by Brother Lawrence
The Sacrament of the Present Moment by Jean-Pierre de Caussade
The Seeking Heart by François Fénelon

2

Life, Wholeness and Healing Flow from Jesus Christ

would like you to consider three important truths.

First, it is essential to recognize that life and wholeness come exclusively from the Person and work of Jesus Christ. There are many instruments of healing available to believers but only one source. Hurting people can find help and guidance as never before from doctors, psychiatrists, psychologists, counselors, friends, self-help books and recovery programs. But Jesus alone has the power to bind the brokenhearted, set the captives free and release people from the prison of emotional and spiritual darkness. Apart from the Lord, professionals, prescriptions and programs offer only short-term relief at best. Through Christ those in emotional and spiritual upheaval can experience a wholeness that goes far deeper than simply eliminating pain and discomfort. Jesus offers the *shalom* of God to all who know and trust in Him. In seasons of crisis you must set your hope in Him as never before.

The second truth is not easy to admit yet is the all-too-common experience of countless Christians. Few men and women press in to know the Lord genuinely until they are faced with suffering and trial. While the language of relationship and friendship with Christ graces witnessing and conversation, all too often it is words without substance. Such shallowness remains hidden so long as life is normal. But in times of crisis, the absence of genuine intimacy with the Lord becomes shockingly obvious.

Your eternal well-being, thankfully, does not depend on your embrace of Christ, but rather on His faithful hold on you. Paul wrote in Romans 8:38–39 that nothing can separate believers from the Lord's love—not even (we may surmise) our own immaturity. That truth is a wonderful comfort, yet it offers no excuse for failing to press in to experience depth and intimacy with Jesus Christ. Knowing about the Lord and serving Him faithfully are not enough to sustain people through a season of darkness. You and I must grow to know Him intimately.

The third truth I want to discuss has been one of the most blessed discoveries of my life. It has affected my entire understanding and experience of day-to-day Christian living, bringing a deep joy I had not previously known. It may not seem profound, but what I discovered was truly transforming: It is possible in this life to have a relationship with Jesus that goes far beyond mere intellectual understanding of historical facts and theological truths. You can experience a real, emotionally fulfilling and spiritually engaging intimacy with Jesus that grows deeper and deeper with time. This, in fact, is the pearl for which one sells all other possessions. Interestingly, many have their first taste of this mystic, sweet relationship during times of great loss and pain. We cry out for Him much more in the dark, it seems, than when surrounded by light.

In the latter part of the seventeenth century, Jeanne Guyon wrote a book about spiritual intimacy. She wanted people to know it is possible to have a deep, inward relationship with Christ. She wrote:

> As you pick up this book, you may feel that you simply are not one of those people capable of a deep experience

with Jesus Christ. Most Christians do not feel that they have been called to a deep, inward relationship to their Lord. But we have all been called to the depths of Christ just as surely as we have been called to salvation.[1]

What Guyon emphasized three hundred years ago needs to be the heart cry of God's people today. We should long to experience an intimate walk with Christ that is tangibly present within our inner being. Such a relationship is not only our privilege, but a necessity in the face of life's uncertainties and demands. When the storm of trial rages, we need Jesus as never before. Jesus Christ is the inexhaustible source of life, healing and wholeness. His riches are unsearchable, discovered over time by those willing to seek Him intimately and love Him passionately.

What follows are several insights and exercises that may help you experience the depths of Jesus, our Lord. For those in the season of suffering and pain, I know of no better pursuit.

Fix Your Eyes on Jesus

God's people must become increasingly consumed with Jesus Christ. Through Him we have every spiritual blessing necessary for life and godliness. This includes not only such benefits as forgiveness of sin, adoption into God's family, reconciliation with the Father and life everlasting, but the strength to walk through the trials and difficulties of life. To be overcomers, we must daily "put on Christ" (Galatians 3:27, KJV) as God's provision for our past, present and future needs.

Jesus Christ is not only the means by which we gain victory in life. He is, in fact, the very "end" or goal of life itself. Paul tells us we were chosen before time to be conformed to the image of Christ: "For those God foreknew he also predestined to be conformed to the likeness of his Son" (Romans 8:29).

Paul is emphasizing that every circumstance we face with Christ forms us to be like Him. As Jesus shows us the way through life, He transforms us to be increasingly like Him in character and behavior. Everything—absolutely everything—about the Christian life rests on Jesus. Is it any wonder that Hebrews 12:2 instructs Christians to fix their gaze on Him? Every eye, and the mind of every believer, must focus continually on the Lord. Such singleness of thought and vision is the necessity and privilege of us all.

Jonathan Edwards, the eighteenth-century American theologian, was a man consumed with Christ. His sermon entitled "Safety, Fullness, and Sweet Refreshment, to Be Found in Christ" is about the wonder of Jesus and His complete provision for believers. Edwards encouraged Christians to find the Lord a refuge from the winds of life, a hiding place when the tempests of trial threaten destruction:

> Christ gives himself to his people to be all things to them that they need, all things that make for their happiness. . . . And that he might be so, he has refused nothing that is needful to prepare him to be so. When it was needful that he should be incarnate, he refused it not, but became a man, and appeared in the form of a servant. When it was needful that he should be slain, he refused it not, but gave himself for us, and gave himself to us upon the cross. Here is love for us to admire, for us to praise, and for us to rejoice in, with joy that is full of glory forever.[2]

Edwards beckons us to be intoxicated joyfully with Jesus Christ. Difficulty, trial and suffering are the very circumstances that produce the insatiable thirst leading to this staggering experience with Him.

A. B. Simpson, a leader in the nineteenth-century revival and missionary movement, and the founder of the Christian and Missionary Alliance, is remembered as a powerful preacher, writer and missionary statesman. But his early Christian experience was marked by failure, frustration and emotional breakdown. In that dark night the Lord revealed Himself to Simpson as his complete sufficiency. All Simpson had to do was surrender fully to Him. Simpson responded and lived a life marked by complete dependence on the Lord. He gave all for Jesus because Jesus was his all.

Throughout his life Simpson challenged believers to give up their lives for the "Christ-life." He wrote:

> Christ-life is a vital and divine experience through the union of the soul with the living Christ Himself. Christian life may be an honest attempt to imitate Christ and follow His teachings and commandments, but Christ-life is the incarnation of Jesus Himself in your own life. It is the Christ reliving His life in you and enabling you to be and to do what, in your own strength, you never could accomplish.[3]

All of us need the Christ-life, and this is never more obvious than in the season of suffering. As such, allow the Holy Spirit to kindle in you a fire of passion for Jesus Christ. The desire to know Him in spirit and truth should consume your life until all other preoccupations are as nothing compared to this one heart cry. There is no better time to cry out than in the dark night, and no more consumable material than the stuff of trial and suffering. By surrender, not striving, you must ask the Spirit to take you to Jesus—and He surely will.

An Approach Worth Considering

Christians today are able to access an unbelievable number of resources about Jesus. There is the testimony not only of Scripture, but of countless books, articles, tapes, movies and videos about Him. Sermons and lectures abound, full of rich insights into His life, works and words. But these alone are not enough if you intend to grow close to the Lord Himself. You must allow the Holy Spirit to shape an intimate, heartfelt relationship with Christ that engages not only your mind, but your spirit and emotions as well.

I believe the following six suggestions may prove helpful in that pursuit.

1. Prayer for Passion

First, ask God to give you a deep passion for Jesus Christ. Let this become a consuming prayer that you lift continually before the throne. Admit that you cannot ignite such a fire on your own, and cry out for the Lord to do what you cannot do in yourself. Persevere in this prayer, asking for a heart like that of the psalmist who wrote, "As the deer pants for streams of water, so my soul pants for you, O God. My soul thirsts for God, for the living God. When can I go and meet with God?" (Psalm 42:1–2).

Pray for a soul that thirsts for Jesus, for a holy preoccupation that keeps you longing for Him and Him alone (see Psalm 63). The Lord loves to answer this prayer. While you may not notice immediate change, this request is perfectly in line with His will. I am convinced that anyone who seeks this desire will, in time, want Jesus more than he or she wants life itself. The passion to know and be with Jesus will be like that of the woman in the Song of Solomon. Intense love caused her to look for her lover, to call out to him, to ask others if they had seen him, and then to give this instruction: "If you find my lover . . . tell him I am faint with love" (Song of Solomon 5:8).

May you be consumed with passion for Christ!

2. Wait in Stillness

Second, whether turning toward Scripture, prayer or reading, learn to wait in stillness before the Lord. Not only is our environment full of sounds and distractions, but we are extremely noisy within ourselves. We have minds given to preoccupations and imaginations, emotions that clamor for attention, bodies demanding care and satisfaction. Put simply, we are loud even when we say nothing.

In contrast, God seeks to move quietly within our spirits. He whispers words of love and comfort, guidance and direction through the Holy Spirit, who abides in every believer. Hearing demands that you get quiet, wait and listen. As you do, the Spirit will quicken you to perceive His voice and enjoy the Lord's manifest presence in your inner being. Such centering is not easily learned, yet is essential to intimacy.

The early leaders of the Christian and Missionary Alliance believed that stillness was an essential discipline of the Christian life. George Pardingdon, a teacher and theologian at the turn of this century, encouraged Christians to wait in silence until the "dew" of God's presence falls. Then and only then can we move on to seek the Lord through Scripture or serve Him in ministry.

Such stillness will open your spirit to see and experience the living Jesus. Your desire for instant gratification must give way to an unhurried rest before the Lord.

3. *Surrender to the Spirit*

Third, approach Scripture, prayer and reading surrendered fully to the Holy Spirit, asking Him to draw you to Christ. Intimacy with Jesus does not come by your own striving. It is a grace gift of God made possible through the Holy Spirit. You and I cannot force, manipulate, earn or acquire such a relationship. Self-effort only gets in the way, keeping us from the union we desire. Instead, surrender and say, "Holy Spirit, would You show me Jesus today as I turn to God's Word? Please draw me to intimacy as I approach Him in prayer. As I read, Holy Spirit, show me the glory of my Lord."

A. B. Simpson, a man for whom I have great admiration, was completely consumed with Jesus Christ. God birthed in him a love for the Lord, and as a result Simpson gave everything he had to Him. Dr. Simpson approached Scripture with a desire to know Christ, and by surrendering to the Holy Spirit he was able to see and experience Jesus on virtually every page. His multi-volume work *Christ in the Bible* is a devotional classic.

If you are hungry to know Christ personally, submit to the Spirit's unveiling of Jesus. He will draw you faithfully into a deeper and more satisfying relationship with the Lord.

4. *Move Slowly*

Fourth, move slowly through Scripture, prayer and reading, seeking to be formed in Christ far more than being informed about the Lord. Most people have been trained by our educational institutions to gather great amounts of knowledge; but knowledge alone does not necessarily produce wisdom, nor in this case does it enhance relationship. Information must be embraced in such a way as to initiate a deep, spiritual transaction within ourselves. Such an encounter has nothing to do with the quality of input, but rather the degree of formation that results. This takes time and requires constant openness to the Holy Spirit.

In the past, since I love to read, I would move quickly through a book, trying to grab all the knowledge I could get. It was critical to my counseling, preaching and teaching, so I took notes on everything important. But when seeking intimacy with Christ, I have learned to approach reading very slowly. Under the Spirit's guidance, I seek to embrace a truth or concept, allowing it to draw me to Jesus. I want to encounter the text (Scripture or otherwise), soaking in its depth rather than skimming over its surface. How long it takes to complete a book does not matter at all. The only thing that counts is seeking and experiencing more of Jesus. This requires restful contemplation and patient meditation on the image or information being considered. I must squeeze out all the "juices" in order to nourish the healthy intimacy I desperately desire.

Recently I read *The Jesus I Never Knew* by Philip Yancey. I approached it in the way I just outlined, and the experience with Christ was transformational. Over and over I would read a page or two and need to stop, wait, listen, meditate and then worship. By my previous standards it seemed to take forever to finish the book. But time matters little when an eternal relationship is being forged.

By slowing down we grow much faster with the Lord.

5. *Open the Imagination*

Fifth, allow the Holy Spirit access to your imagination, so you can visualize a particular truth, event or image relating to the Lord. This approach will open you to Jesus in ways that go beyond your mind, engaging your senses and emotions at deep and powerful levels. I have found this a revolutionizing experience, helping me enter a text or truth in ways I never accessed by an information-based process.

One day I was meditating on the crucifixion account in John 19. The Holy Spirit quickened me to "enter" the event through my imagination. Slowly I began to visualize the many details surrounding Calvary. As I began to focus on the Lord being nailed to the cross, an emotional response began that was powerful, almost frightening. Love and gratitude for the Lord began to pour from my heart while tears streamed down my face. The sacrifice of Christ became more real than ever before as I "watched" Him die for me. The sense of His presence surrounded me and continued for several days. I found myself consumed with Jesus and quickened deeply to know Him more intimately.

Robert Mulholland, professor of New Testament at Asbury Theological Seminary, encourages this technique as a key discipline for spiritual reading. In his book *Shaped by the Word* he writes:

> You imagine the things you would be seeing . . . the things you would be hearing . . . smelling . . . feeling. . . . You use all your senses. You let your imagination loose to recreate the setting of the passage of Scripture. Once you have recreated the scene, then begin to examine your thoughts and feelings about the situation. You may experience harmony/dissonance. This can become a focus for your prayerful openness to God.[4]

6. Worship the Lord

Once you have slowly and sensitively "entered" some truth regarding Christ, and been quickened by the Holy Spirit to behold Him, the time now comes for you to be still in His presence and worship. This worship is not necessarily characterized by any observable activity, such as singing or praying (though it can be). It is an inward communion and adoration that engages the spirit, an awakening of an intimate presence of Christ that is present deep within your being. At such times you will realize that the Lord is not sitting on some transcendent throne, but reigning within your heart. New love for Jesus is born, and your relationship with Him takes on a dynamic quality of oneness.

These encounters not only enhance intimacy but place the issues of your life in divine perspective. In Christ's presence, agonies and difficulties just do not matter as much. He is the Treasure of life, and in having Him you have all things. The pain may still be there, or the trial or need. But His presence overrides it all in importance. Moments such as these are not about expending much energy trying to solve or overcome or escape a problem. Spiritual rest enters your inner being, and your central motivation is for more of Jesus. A new strength enters your weakness, and striving gives way to peace—His peace.

Madame Guyon encouraged the believers of her day repeatedly to grow in Christ. In her classic work *Experiencing the Depths of Jesus Christ*, she wrote:

> The Lord's chief desire is to reveal Himself to you and in order for Him to do that, He gives you abundant grace. The Lord gives you the experience of enjoying His presence. He touches you, and His touch is so delightful that, more than ever, you are drawn inwardly to Him.[5]

Knowing Christ is your greatest need and most invaluable privilege. No other focus of life is even remotely worthy of consideration. Never is this more obvious than when the storms of life threaten to capsize your life. You need Jesus. Not just His words and works—you need Jesus Himself. You need to be consumed in Him, the hope of glory. With Paul you must cry out,

> I want to know Christ and the power of his resurrection and the fellowship of sharing in his sufferings, becoming like him in his death, and so, somehow, to attain to the resurrection from the dead.
>
> Philippians 3:10–11

The Unsearchable Riches of Christ

Scripture abounds with the images, truths and teachings of Christ. Whether Old Testament prophecies, gospels or epistles, you can feast on countless passages that draw you into the Lord's presence. In his letter to the Ephesian church, Paul refers to "the unsearchable riches of Christ" (Ephesians 3:8). I believe this phrase demands attention.

Read and reread the first three chapters of that epistle, taking a red pen and underlining each reference that speaks of a benefit that is yours in Him. Make a list of each benefit of Christ listed in Ephesians 1–3, similar to the list that follows:

Holiness	Chosen
Blamelessness	Sealing by the Spirit
Adoption	Spirit of wisdom
Glorious grace	and revelation
Redemption	Hope
Forgiveness of sin	Great power
Salvation	Life
Seated in the heavenlies	Nearness to God
Peace	Access to the Father
Knowledge of God's will	Unity with other believers

Christ within, who is able
to do immeasurably more
than I ask or imagine

Love of Christ
Spiritual dwelling

This list can become the focus of your contemplative prayer. Under the Spirit's guidance, embrace these truths one at a time according to the steps suggested earlier. While it may take time, the effects will be invaluable. Hope, faith and love for Jesus will begin to fill the wounds that the season of suffering exposed. Like fuel to a fire, each benefit will serve to ignite a greater passion to know this wonderful Savior. The nourishment such contemplation brings will feed your soul, enhancing growth and spiritual vitality. A deep, spiritual transaction will occur whenever you meditate on the eternal riches that are yours in Christ Jesus.

The Incomparable Work of Christ

I have a strange habit that people ask me about continually: I write on the palm of my hand. I am not sure when it began, but every day I note some abbreviated biblical truth that is to be the focus of my attention. I do this at the close of my quiet time, jotting down some phrase or symbol that will help me center on the Lord's truth. Most of what I note varies, but without fail I write these letters on my hand every day: *I, C, R, G, P.* They stand for *incarnation, crucifixion, resurrection, glorification* and *Pentecost.*

Early on in my journey through night, I was compelled to spend time contemplating the various aspects of Christ's work, divided according to the categories listed above. One by one I soaked in the truth of what each one means to the believer. The Holy Spirit illumined my mind, touched my emotions and quickened my spirit. He drew me into a new dimension of the presence of Christ, each aspect of His work unfolding before me. There I waited, listened and worshiped.

The following discussion is necessarily brief. But if a believer moves toward each aspect of the work of Christ slowly, still before the Lord, surrendered to the Spirit with an open imagination, the potential for growth in intimacy is limitless.

Incarnation

Meditating on the incarnation reveals that regardless of the circumstance or suffering, Jesus has been there. He knows the power of temptation, the pain of rejection and the agony of physical suffering. He understands abuse, has battled through despair and experienced the sorrow and grief of losing a loved one to death. The Lord sympathizes with you in your weakness and moves toward you with great compassion, totally free of condemnation.

When I talk to people who have experienced major depression, we have immediate rapport. We understand each other as only fellow pilgrims can, bringing a sense of comfort and emotional unity. What a joy to discover that Jesus, more than anyone else, understands the fellowship of suffering! You can and must turn to Him without fear of clichés and pat answers. Jesus knows what it is like to suffer and He moves in tenderly to bring strength, hope and healing to your life.

Crucifixion

Jesus' crucifixion is the death that is your only hope for life. He died your death on the cross so that you could experience His life. Contemplating the cross is a forever privilege and will draw you into Christ as little else. The debt is canceled; the payment has been made in full.

Satan is defeated, God is satisfied and you have been redeemed. Jesus finished the work at the price of His blood . . . for you.

When you are battling the staggering effects of brokenness, considering His wounds brings more than hope; it brings healing. Isaiah 53:5 reads, "By his wounds we are healed." This means not only His physical wounds, but His emotional, mental and spiritual wounds as well—Christ's complete brokenness for your complete healing. Jesus was impaled to the cross so you could walk free. Meditating on this will inspire hope, enhance intimacy and ignite heartfelt worship and praise. In addition, by the Spirit's presence, healing results!

Resurrection

You are not what you once were. While many of your behaviors may contradict this claim, it is true just the same. Your old, sinful nature was crucified with Christ at Calvary. That unholy, unrighteous, independent, rebellious core of being was put to death. Even though you may not have surrendered to the Spirit's sanctifying work in every area of your life, that sinful nature is gone. In its place is the glorious, holy, righteous, obedient nature of Christ. The resurrection power of Jesus has transformed you to the very heart of your being, and you are by nature like Him. Though staggering, this is eternally true!

I love to contemplate the promise of the resurrection. Many of my emotional problems stemmed from self-rejection. Abhorred by the darkness and depravity of my life, I sought to compensate through performance and striving. Feelings of shame deep inside drove me to become a better person, and the pursuit wore me out.

What a joy to learn that you are not what you were! Jesus has changed all that. Discovering who you are in Him will transform your self-perception. This in turn will affect your relationships, responses and priorities. Meditating on your new identity brings new freedom and an explosion of gratitude and praise. This concept is so vital to well-being that a more complete discussion follows in chapter 10. Remember, Jesus gives you new, resurrection life!

Glorification

The apostle Paul taught that our battle is not against flesh and blood (see Ephesians 6:12). Instead Christians war with evil principalities and powers hell-bent on our destruction. These dark spirits seek to harass, oppress and afflict believers in countless ways, both covert and obvious. On our own we would be powerless—vulnerable victims of their violent schemes.

Look once again to Jesus Christ. His victory over evil was your victory. He did not die to give Himself power over Satan, for Jesus had that from eternity past. Christ won so that you can now win. He has given you authority over the power of darkness. Granted, you may have much to learn about exercising this right, but it is yours just the same.

Jesus Christ has been glorified, now enthroned above all powers and dominion. And, as Paul taught in Ephesians 2:6, we are seated with Him in the heavenlies. This glorification is where you must take your stand, by faith, against Satan. What joy and encouragement to know you are not a helpless victim. Because of Christ, you are a conqueror, and more.

Every day meditate on this truth. Visualize its implications for your life, and be quickened by the Spirit to recognize and resist the evil one. When you fail, you need only take your stand with Christ once again and move on to overcome. The glorification of Christ is your glorification, too—a wondrous work of grace that brings about, yet again, more love and more surrender to the Lord.

Pentecost

Before Jesus ascended to heaven, He made a promise to send the Holy Spirit to help His disciples. Recognizing and responding to His presence is vital to your well-being and growth. The Spirit's power and strength make all the difference between victory and defeat, particularly when the path you face is difficult and dark. This topic is so important that I have given the entire next chapter over to it.

Years ago churches sang a chorus entitled "He's Everything to Me." Although the song is no longer popular, the truth is eternal and relevant to us all. Jesus Christ is the full answer to life now and forever. His riches are unsearchable, His works incomparable and His ways indescribable.

Astounding as He is, the Lord still invites you to know Him intimately. He calls out to bring you near, beckoning you to come and find light and comfort in the glow of His presence. Will you draw close to the fire?

For Further Reading

Experiencing the Depths of Jesus Christ by Madame Guyon
The Christ-life by A. B. Simpson
Life in Christ by John R.W. Stott
The Kiss of Intimacy by Andy and Jane Fitz-Gibbon
The Jesus I Never Knew by Philip Yancey
The Signature of Jesus by Brennan Manning

3

The Holy Spirit Is Always Present with You

More than once I have been asked to identify the most important change that has occurred in my life as a result of my dark night. This is not an easy question to answer, because in many ways my life was literally transformed. Patterns of behavior have changed, as well as priorities, values and many aspects of my lifestyle. Most important, my relationship with God has taken on a dimension that is refreshing and powerful. The journey, though painful and at times frightening, resulted in a kind of new birth experience. Many things have passed away in their significance, while countless others have been made new.

But if pressed to highlight a single discovery that catches my attention first and foremost, I would have to cite my relationship with the Holy Spirit. Along the pathway of suffering, the Spirit revealed Himself to me as I had never before seen or understood. The reality of His immanence became tangible. A dimension of Spirit-directed and Spirit-filled living unfolded before me that, to this day, influences my entire understanding of the Christian walk.

The Person and work of the Holy Spirit had been a theological reality to me even before I surrendered to

Christ. But as a Christian, I related to Him predominantly in cognitive awareness, not as ongoing spirit to Spirit. Certainly there were times and seasons when I felt His presence, power and anointing. Yet daily living was directed by my own agenda or that of others around me, and much of my thinking was rooted in carnality (albeit religious carnality) absent of true life and power. The me that needed to die was very much alive and in control, quenching the activity of the Holy Spirit and numbing me to His life-giving presence and direction. But as the dark night invited more and more death, the voice of the Spirit became clearer and stronger. As I weakened my stranglehold on life, He laid hold of me as never before.

Paul told the Corinthians that "the Lord is the Spirit, and where the Spirit of the Lord is, there is freedom" (2 Corinthians 3:17). I have learned that every moment I surrender to His Lordship, I am free to embrace that indescribable gift of Spirit life. And so are you.

The Church of Jesus Christ is experiencing a movement of God's Holy Spirit unprecedented in human history. While the Spirit has been active and involved since creation, the intensity, breadth and observable nature of His outpouring on earth today are fantastic! While the streams seem varied, each flows out of the mighty river of His activity, sweeping across people like a torrent.

Last year I listened in awe as two college students visited our community and told of a revival outbreak on many campuses in the United States. Open confession of sin and repentance characterized the movement, and countless lives were being changed.

A few months later men from our church went to Promise Keepers. The Holy Spirit fell, and as a result lives are being deeply and lastingly rearranged. The Spirit's work through Promise Keepers is increasing every day.

Last summer my family and I stopped in Toronto to see and experience an amazing outpouring of the Holy Spirit. While some manifestations are unfamiliar and in some cases unbiblical, the work of God there is unquestionable. Each of us was affected profoundly by what went on, as much of the world has been.

More recently a nationally recognized leader in the prayer movement spoke at our church, sharing stories of the Holy Spirit igniting people to pray as never before. Momentum is building in anticipation of a great renewal.

These are but four streams of the Spirit's ministry that are moving on people today. Different in expression and appeal, each ushers men and women into a new and more radical dimension of Christian discipleship. And in this age of unmanageable stress, increasing demand and pervasive evil, life in the Holy Spirit is the only real way to experience peace.

My Turning Point

Let there be no mistake about it: I would never have made it through my own season of suffering without the presence of the Holy Spirit in my life. I am not talking about having a theological understanding that He was resident within me. That alone would never have held me fast. I am speaking of a tangible experience of His help and comfort that held me together when, by all other signs, I was sure to fall apart. The Holy Spirit made Himself real to me in the darkness and became the one sustaining Presence to whom I turned repeatedly. He revealed His nearness as I had never known it before, and whenever I surrendered to His control, He led me step by step through the maze of trial. Still horribly difficult and often frightening, the journey also brought peace and meaning with Him as my Friend and Guide.

It was not always like that. In the earliest days of the difficult journey, I felt alone and abandoned. Thoughts of hopelessness and fear ran rampant, wearing me down with emotional fatigue. I faced a void that seemed godless and a power to destructive thinking that overwhelmed me. But with one Scripture and one prayer, everything began to change.

I turned to my Bible one day, in a time of great turmoil, for some direction. As I read Romans 8:6, the Holy Spirit illuminated a great truth to my mind: "The mind of sinful man is death, but the mind controlled by the Spirit is life and peace." It was suddenly so clear, so obvious. The fact that I had no life and peace meant only one thing: I was controlled by my own thinking, not the Holy Spirit. Seeing this, I turned by faith to God and confessed that my carnal mind was in control, full of lies and hopelessness. I admitted that the mind I once took pride in was now in fact destroying my life. Claiming the promise that Jesus died to set me free of the flesh, I prayerfully reckoned my mind as dead with Christ at the cross (see Romans 6:11). Then I said, "Holy Spirit, I do not want *my* mind; I want the mind of Christ. Please take over my thinking that I might have life and peace. I want Christ's thoughts, not mine, and I surrender to Your control."

At that instant I felt the Holy Spirit stir deep within. A surge of life and hope energized me, and for a moment I was free. His presence was so real and tangible that a sense of joy rose up from my inner being, and for a time I was reconnected with the Lord. It did not last all that long at first, but a genuine transaction took place. From that moment until this, I have turned repeatedly to that same Scripture and prayer. Sometimes, when the battle was great, I prayed it a thousand times in a day. At other times I was able to rest for longer seasons in the peace of the Holy Spirit's presence. But either way the Holy

Spirit quickened me deep inside each time I turned, by faith, to His control.

Before long a new dependence and relationship with the Holy Spirit began to be forged. My trial became the context of spiritual growth and maturity. The Holy Spirit showed me that He is always there, deep within my being, as a river of living water. As I surrendered my mind to Him, the Spirit centered my thinking faithfully on the truth of God's love and great mercy. This initiated the peace and life I desperately needed in order to press on in the journey. And each time, step by step, the Holy Spirit made His presence more real to my life.

The Holy Spirit and Seasons of Trial

In time I learned there was a great deal the Holy Spirit wanted to bring to this season. He showed Himself as the Spirit of fellowship, strength, truth, comfort, hope, teaching, empowerment and freedom. These aspects of the Spirit's work have been so important in my journey that I want to discuss them briefly here. Everyone facing trial and suffering, I believe, can benefit wonderfully from His ministry. Ultimately we learn that the greatest joy is simply communing in His presence. There, trial or ease, poverty or abundance, pain or pleasure do not matter as much. He, the Holy Spirit of Christ, becomes enough.

And, my friend, He is always there, more accessible than you could ever imagine. The Holy Spirit is God within us, abiding faithfully in the interior throne room of our lives. We need only turn there in surrender and stillness to discover the wonder of our divine Helper and Friend.

What follows is a brief yet important discussion of the Holy Spirit's ministry to the broken and struggling believer. I am choosing to use illustrations from my difficult journey because they represent the real-life context of my own growth in the Spirit. The issues are often the same, however, for every pilgrim seeking freedom during a season of trial and darkness.

The Spirit of Fellowship

The dark night of the soul, no matter what form it takes, can be a time of loneliness. Most people do not understand what it is like or how deep the pain and despair can be. Their hearts are right, wanting to help, but their clichés and quick-fix solutions often bring more frustration than relief. I remember, at a time of great difficulty, being sent fifty dollars by a friend. He told me to get myself some gift that would make me feel better. On the one hand I was deeply touched, yet on the other hand heartsick that he thought money would help. I felt very alone in it all.

Loneliness and abandonment debilitate a person. Such feelings settle in like a cold, dark oppression. I often asked my wife to stay home with me when this battle raged, just to avoid the emotional struggle. But once, at a time of significant loneliness, I sensed the Lord challenging me to press in to the feelings rather than escape from them. Apprehensive, I began cautiously to pray, asking the Lord to teach me something through the pain. What I discovered shocked me. The Lord showed me that loneliness could actually be a doorway to fellowship with the Holy Spirit.

When such feelings began, I was to turn to the Spirit for companionship and intimacy. Whenever the darkness threatened, I was to be more deliberate about drawing near to the fire of His presence. At first it was awkward, but soon I actually felt Him breaking through the cloud of abandonment. He taught me through Scripture that He was always present within, accessible through faith and prayer. I suddenly realized that I was never alone, even in times of isolation and solitude. I found that at any moment I surrendered to His help, He was tangibly there deep within.

Fellowship with the Holy Spirit is rich and meant for you. This relationship, though often enhanced through trial, is to become part of your day-to-day Christian life. He wants you to enjoy His presence, communing continually through prayer and worship. The Holy Spirit is present within you and longs to make Himself known to hungry and thirsty followers of Christ. He is a real Person willing to enter into a marvelous friendship with you if you will only seek Him. Like any relationship, it takes time and regular encounters with the Spirit. But before long you will find increasing intimacy and joy in the Holy Spirit's presence.

A. W. Tozer encouraged believers to get to know the Holy Spirit at deeper and deeper levels. He wrote:

> The Holy Spirit is a living Person, and we can know Him and fellowship with Him! . . . Walking with the Spirit can become a habit. It is a gracious thing to strive to know the things of God through the Spirit of God in a friendship that passes the place where it has to be kept up by chatter.[1]

Fellowship with the Holy Spirit is a precious gift offered to every follower of Christ. I have come to be thankful for the very loneliness I once feared, for it led me to the One who is always there.

The Strength of the Holy Spirit

Countless times during the more than two decades I have been involved in Christian service, I have prayed before ministering, asking for the Holy Spirit's help and anointing. But in truth, most of the time I was self-confident about what I was doing. Whether it was preaching, teaching or administrating, I always knew things would be fine. I had good health and an adequate mind, so most tasks came with relative ease and generally turned out well. People often affirmed me in my work, so I was comfortable in ministry.

All of that changed radically (as you can imagine) in 1992. One of the lingering effects of my dark night was unbelievable fear. In reaction to all the emotional upheaval, I became practically homebound. Everything I once counted on as my source of strength failed me. My physical and emotional health slipped, and I no longer trusted the mind I had once relied on. I felt weak and vulnerable at every front.

After three months of isolation, it came time for me to return to work. Things I once relished and found important were now places of great struggle. The thought of preaching or teaching caused me to break out in a cold sweat. All my self-confidence was gone and I was scared to death. But, as with all else, this trial was a place of learning.

The Lord showed me how proud and arrogant I had become. Achievement and responsibility made me feel important and needed. God also revealed that my self-reliance was unacceptable as a basis of ministry. Through extreme weakness He taught me to rest completely on the strength of the Holy Spirit. I now had to pray for hours before ministering, asking for the Spirit's help and anointing. On countless occasions I stood to speak feeling undone and incapable, yet each time He came and used me in the moment of service. At a season in my life when I felt I had nothing to offer, God moved through me as never before. And it was all Him!

Today I no longer feel the fear I once did. But I have learned, I hope, to stay in the place of weakness, resting on the Spirit's strength, not my own. My role is to remain humble and dependent before Him. The Holy Spirit is the One who makes the difference in people's lives. I am just a channel.

The prophet Isaiah said, "In quietness and trust is your strength" (Isaiah 30:15). I believe that now. As we quiet ourselves from pride and self-reliance, the Holy Spirit can bring incredible strength to the moment. You may be in a very trying time as you read this book. Possibly you are battling weakness as you have never known. Bless it! For right now you can find the Spirit's strength for your life and learn a new kind of confidence: Spirit confidence.

The Spirit of Truth

In the gospel of John we find these important words from Jesus regarding the Holy Spirit:

> "If you love me, you will obey what I command. And I will ask the Father, and he will give you another Counselor to be with you forever—the Spirit of truth."
>
> John 14:15–17

The relationship between truth and personal freedom is critical—so much so that I have given the entire next chapter to this topic. Much of the difficulty Christians experience is rooted in deception, sin and deep wounding. It is essential that we see the truth of what is going on in our lives so we can repent accordingly and seek healing. These issues must be addressed thoroughly if God's people are to be released from the chains that keep us enslaved and move on to claim our new identities in Christ Jesus.

This task is far too great, frankly, for human resources alone. It takes the ongoing work of the Holy Spirit, who faithfully reveals the truth to any Christian willing to surrender to His work. Know this: True freedom does not come because some counselor analyzed our emotional issues, then helped us modify our behavior accordingly. Revelation, release and restoration are activities of God's Spirit. He often uses a caregiver as a channel of His work, but remember that it is the Holy Spirit who truly counsels and delivers. You must surrender to His activity in order to get to the root issues of your brokenness.

Several years ago my friend Amanda Hunt entered her own dark night. She was absolutely clueless as to how and why she got there. Hoping to escape, she turned to some professional caregivers for help. Although some of their analysis was relevant, it was clear to Amanda that their approach lacked something. That something was, in fact, Someone, who could pinpoint every issue needing change or healing in her life. Turning to Spirit-filled and Spirit-directed counselors made all the difference. They helped her move beyond analysis to divine action.

The Holy Spirit revealed to Amanda hidden sin, false beliefs and deep wounds that were destroying her life. She did not have to sweat and strain, trying to remember or find something to confess. The Holy Spirit was specific and amazingly clear. Amanda needed only to stay surrendered to His sanctifying presence. Granted, it took time, but there was little mystery to what He wanted her to address.

The Holy Spirit also revealed to Amanda important truths regarding the promises and provisions of Christ for her life. Primarily He taught Amanda about God's deep love and acceptance and the truth about who she was in Christ. These biblical principles brought healing to her inner being and helped her release a very dysfunctional lifestyle.

There is no counselor like the Spirit of truth. As you cry out for His help, the Holy Spirit moves to reveal every inconsistency and deception that hinders your life. He does this lovingly yet honestly, all with the goal of your freedom. If you simply turn and cry out, "Show me," the Holy Spirit of truth will move to uncover sin, expose lies, heal wounds and restore well-being to your life.

The Spirit of Comfort

When Jesus told His followers He was going to send the Holy Spirit to them, He called the Spirit the *paraclete* (John 14:16). This word is rich and full of meaning, including such concepts as *Counselor, Helper* and *Comforter.* Jesus wanted to leave no doubt about the many-faceted role the Holy Spirit would play in the believer's life. Jesus knew the world would bring trouble, and He did not want to leave us to struggle all alone. In times of trial, Christians do well to understand and embrace every aspect of the Spirit's presence. Particular to seasons of pain and difficulty is His ministry of comfort.

Anyone who has experienced the dark night knows very well the times of great heartache and loss along the way. I struggled with both of these feelings and am confident that I would have spiraled into a black hole of despair had it not been for the comfort of the Holy Spirit. When the turmoil was greatest, He moved on me with incredible love and compassion. The Holy Spirit was there to bring peace and rest to my weary and downcast soul. Sometimes too weak even to pray, I felt His help well up within. It was just as Paul said: "The Spirit himself [interceding] for us with groans that words cannot express" (Romans 8:26).

I prayed with Ed Turner while he struggled through a season of deep weeping as he faced childhood realities. He grieved in particular for not having had an intimate relationship with his father. For years Ed had struggled with feelings of being unwanted by his dad, but had stuffed the hurt and ignored the deep wounds. Now, as Ed considered all that had resulted from his dad's lack of involvement in his life, and all the missed opportunities to build intimacy, his heart broke and a flood of tears and pain poured out from his inner being.

After weeping in great sorrow for some time, Ed said he felt empty and quite undone. It was then that he began to sense the presence of the Holy Spirit moving in to fill the void and bring healing. The Spirit's gentleness and compassion were overwhelming. The Holy Spirit understood his pain, Ed told me, and comforted him in such a tangible way that peace and joy began to well up inside. He suddenly knew he was truly loved and accepted by his heavenly Father. This truth brought a new wholeness to Ed's life and enabled him to turn and extend genuine forgiveness to his father.

You are not alone in your heartache. The Holy Spirit stands ever ready to comfort you in the midst of pain and loss. He cares and comes to all who mourn, willing to bring peace in the midst of turmoil and joy through all the sorrow. You need only turn in faith and the Holy Spirit will be there, even in your darkest hour, longing to comfort and bring hope to your life.

The Spirit of Hope

Judy McClure called and asked if I would please spend some time with her husband, John. He was battling depression and she feared he was about to give up. Well acquainted with those feelings, I agreed to meet with John. As soon as our eyes met, he began to weep. His emotions were frayed and John was desperate. His first words to me were, "Terry, I've lost all hope. All I want to do is end it all."

Several years earlier I had been in a similar place. Frightened, wondering if my mind was at serious risk and unsure if I would ever regain stability, I had talked to my wife about plans in case of possible institutionalization. Questions like *How long will this last?* and *How bad will it get?* haunted me. All I saw was a bottomless pit and felt I was falling fast.

The day John came to see me, I took him to the very Scriptures that had helped me hold on through the darkness. He needed that one quality that would keep him going, as it had me: hope. I opened my Bible and began to read to him:

> May the God of hope fill you with all joy and peace as you trust in him, so that you may overflow with hope by the power of the Holy Spirit.
>
> Romans 15:13

> The God of all grace, who called you to his eternal glory in Christ, after you have suffered a little while, will himself restore you and make you strong, firm and steadfast.
>
> 1 Peter 5:10

Then we went to the Lord in prayer and asked Him to make these promises a deep inner conviction within John's spirit. Wonderfully the Holy Spirit moved in our midst, and at that moment began to turn the situation around. The Spirit instilled hope in John and strengthened him to hold on.

People who struggle in life need hope. Without it all desire fades and despair sets in to destroy. Hope instills new energy, inspires trust in God's deliverance and encourages us to make it through another day.

Such hope is not the result of positive thinking. It comes as a transaction of the Holy Spirit in the life of the believer. It pushes back the clouds of gloom and pessimism, bringing the light of God's promised deliverance and restoration. Hope serves as an anchor in the storm, tethering believers to the Lord's love and mercy. You can access this wonderful ministry of the Holy Spirit by the prayer of faith, even when your faith is the size of a mustard seed. You need but turn to Him, laying hold of these Scriptures as a promise. And each time you cry out, the Holy Spirit will come and whisper gently, "This, too, shall pass. Hold on."

The Holy Spirit as Our Teacher

Most often we spend time in the valley because we are living by misplaced priorities and unbiblical principles. God allows us to enter the dark with the intention of bringing new light and direction into our lives. If we are open, the Holy Spirit will instruct us clearly and carefully in the way of the Lord. He will show us where we are unbalanced and misguided, then teach us to live according to the truth.

There is no question but that I had embraced an unhealthy understanding of the Christian life. But to tell you the truth, I did not have a clue how far off I really was. My priorities were thoroughly religious and consistent with what I saw in virtually every leader in my life. And to make matters worse, I was affirmed and rewarded repeatedly for my approach to ministry. But God made it clear through my breakdown that my understanding of dynamic discipleship did not match His. On realizing the depth of my deception, I asked the Holy Spirit to teach me Christ's way and then to help me truly live by it. And for several years now He has been answering that prayer.

Jesus spoke to His disciples about the Holy Spirit and made repeated references to the Spirit teaching believers all truth. Below are a few such references from the gospels:

> "When you are brought before synagogues, rulers and authorities, do not worry about how you will defend

yourselves or what you will say, for the Holy Spirit will teach you at that time what you should say."

Luke 12:11–12

"The Counselor, the Holy Spirit, whom the Father will send in my name, will teach you all things and will remind you of everything I have said to you."

John 14:26

"When he, the Spirit of truth, comes, he will guide you into all truth."

John 16:13

If you are willing and open, the Holy Spirit will illumine your heart to the principles of God. He will reveal truth in the Word and guide you to new understanding of the priorities of biblical living.

Opening yourself to the instruction of the Holy Spirit will reshape your life. He will teach you that intimacy, not ministry, is to be the consuming passion of the believer. He will show you that solitude and prayer accomplish more in the Kingdom than programs and performance ever will. The Holy Spirit will instruct you about the power of rest, the strength of quiet and the priority of waiting before the Lord. Countless precepts, as ancient as Scripture itself, will come to you new and fresh through the tutelage of the Holy Spirit. Whether through Scripture, sermon, book or brother, His voice of instruction can be heard if only you learn to listen. And listen you must, if you hope to grow beyond the present struggles that weigh you down.

The Spirit of Empowerment

I will probably never forget praying for Dennis Carter at an area pastors' meeting. The theme of the discussion that day was "Life in the Holy Spirit." The speaker discussed a great revival breaking out in Latin America. He told of a powerful outpouring of the Spirit on leaders, transforming their lives and ministries. At the close of the meeting, the area coordinator invited people to receive prayer, and for some reason asked me to minister with him. So without much warning, there I was standing next to Dennis, a pastor who was asking to receive special prayer.

I asked Dennis how I might pray for him, and his response was familiar. He spoke of frustration, fatigue and general disillusionment with his ministry and relationship with the Lord. Pastoring had grown especially hard, Dennis said, and prayer for him was consistently dry. As a result of all this, he was at the end of his rope. His final words before beginning to pray were, "There just has to be more, or I cannot go on."

There *is* more! The Lord Jesus gave the Holy Spirit at Pentecost to empower His people. He even warned the disciples to wait for the Spirit before launching out in ministry (see Acts 1:4), knowing that service without power is unwise and ineffective. Yet countless men and women attempt to live the Christian life without the ongoing infilling of the Holy Spirit. Though born of the Spirit, people go on to live the Christian life by the flesh, and it just does not work. Listen to the apostle Paul: "Are you so foolish? After beginning with the Spirit, are you now trying to attain your goal by human effort?" (Galatians 3:3). Human striving after righteousness only leads to more and more bondage. Countless believers experience despair and burnout precisely because they have not experienced the empowerment of Pentecost in their own lives.

This infilling is more than mental assent to doctrine. It is an experience of God's power that transforms daily living and Christian service. It is a fullness that brings unusual authority, effectiveness and intimacy into one's life. And through prayer and surrender, it can be an ongoing and repeatable encounter with God that brings continual renewal and refreshing. This is why Paul commanded Christians to be filled with the Holy Spirit (see Ephesians 5:18). All believers need this fullness.

I suggest several steps to seeking His touch.[2]

1. Admit to yourself that you need the Holy Spirit's fullness in your life.
2. Prayerfully review the biblical teaching on being filled with the Holy Spirit.
3. Ask the Holy Spirit to identify any hindrances in you that may be blocking His work, such as unconfessed sin, unbelief, fear or broken relationships.
4. Seek out people with whom the Holy Spirit is moving in power, spending time under the anointing of His presence.
5. Pray to receive the Holy Spirit's infilling, trusting that God loves to answer persistent prayer (see Luke 11:5–13).

I believe God touches men and women hungering for more of His Spirit. Just ask Dennis Carter. It has been six months now since we prayed. I received a note from him yesterday in which he wrote that the effects of that day of prayer are continuing to change his life. That is a sure sign that the Holy Spirit is at work!

The Spirit of Freedom

When the Holy Spirit moves on a life, He can accomplish more in a moment than we could in a month of counseling sessions! If you want freedom, seek His presence and touch above all else.

I had met with Steve Spencer several times regarding his in-laws. For years their relationship was strained, and most recently they were not speaking. Though they are all believers, the enemy had secured a powerful stronghold of bitterness and anger between them. I had talked to Steve repeatedly about forgiveness and reconciliation, as had many of his Christian friends, but it was to no avail. Steve had been hurt deeply and repeatedly, and his anger was now a way of protecting himself. He would not budge and things were getting worse.

One night Steve and his wife, Chris, came to a prayer group where the Holy Spirit was moving in power. At one point he stood for prayer, and I watched as he was touched powerfully by the Spirit's presence. Almost instantly he turned to his wife, said something and left the meeting. I thought he was either upset or frightened somehow. The truth was, the Holy Spirit called Steve to repentance and reconciliation. He went to his in-laws immediately and sought their forgiveness, confessing with deep regret his resentment and anger. In a moment the Holy Spirit accomplished a needed work of healing in that family.

I firmly believe that lasting freedom is a work of the Holy Spirit—so much so that my entire approach to counseling has changed. If I have an afternoon of appointments, I spend the morning in prayer as preparation. Since the Holy Spirit is the real Counselor, I want to be in tune with His purposes for each person. I wait in prayer for any words of direction or revelation that will help their situation. During the session I listen to the people but try to stay tuned even more to the Spirit. I give as much as half the time to ministering prayer. All this is based on my belief that one moment in God's presence can change a life.

Spirit-directed counseling is critical. So is soaking in the Holy Spirit's presence. He alone, not wise words or clever analysis, brings true freedom and deliverance. If you need help, guidance, healing and wholeness, seek the Spirit, who sets people free. He can bring release to the deepest bondages of our lives. The Holy Spirit is able to restore the health once stolen by years of abuse and neglect. Sometimes He works in a moment, at other times over a long process. But it is His work that makes the critical difference.

Yes, I believe receiving counsel and spiritual direction from gifted men and women is important. But they can help you only to the degree that the Holy Spirit works in and through their ministries. His touch is what you need, so seek Him first and foremost—but most assuredly in the day of trial. Remember the words of Paul: "The Lord is the Spirit, and where the Spirit of the Lord is, there is freedom" (2 Corinthians 3:17).

A Final Word of Warning

I trust you are convinced that the Holy Spirit is indispensable to spiritual well-being. Possibly He has even used this chapter to inspire you to seek Him more than ever before. I hope so, for life in the Spirit is both exciting and fulfilling. In a world of trouble and trial, His presence is the only way to stand firm.

You must also realize that it is possible to hinder the activity of the Holy Spirit. He does not move freely on those who are either unprepared or unwilling to receive His ministry. It is important that we search our hearts faithfully for any and all barriers that might restrict the Holy Spirit's activity within our lives, including:

Lack of Understanding

Many evangelical Christians have an underdeveloped view of the Holy Spirit's ministry. Careful review of biblical material can open our hearts to exciting truths about His presence and power for living.

Unbelief

More than once Jesus linked unbelief to spiritual poverty. The scientific age has shaped our understanding of reality, robbing people of spiritual life. Faith in the Holy Spirit's presence is a prerequisite to spiritual power. We must believe He is living and active in our world in order to experience His transforming touch.

Fear

In 1 Thessalonians 5:19 Paul admonishes believers, "Do not put out the Spirit's fire." The Holy Spirit is at times a most uncomfortable Comforter! He stretches us beyond our comfort zones and moves in ways far beyond our understanding. Sometimes we try to control the Holy Spirit out of fear, quenching His work. Using Scripture as our guide, we must allow Him room to move in our midst with power.

Unconfessed Sin

In Ephesians 4:30–31 Paul warns Christians not to grieve the Holy Spirit. Then he lists numerous sins as unacceptable actions that stifle His work. Relational sin is particularly problematic and must be addressed if we hope to experience the outpouring of His presence.

Unbalanced Priorities

Intimacy with the Lord must be first and foremost in our lives. Any substitute restricts the activity of the Holy Spirit. His primary ministry is that of testifying to the

Lord Christ and working out the freedom that Jesus accomplished for us on Calvary.

Lack of Persistence

The Lord promised the Holy Spirit to those who hunger and thirst after Him. Persistence and perseverance are often the signs of that deep desire. Countless believers give up too quickly, growing weary before the breakthrough. But those who persist in asking, seeking and knocking are promised the life and power of the Holy Spirit.

On the Mount of Olives Jesus instructed His followers to wait for the Holy Spirit. His promised presence was to be for them the key to life and ministry. As it was for them, so it is now for you. Will you join me in praying, "Come, Holy Spirit"?

For Further Reading

The Counselor by A. W. Tozer
The Acts of the Holy Spirit by A. B. Simpson
Surprised by The Holy Spirit by Jack Deere
The Holy Spirit by Billy Graham
When the Spirit Comes with Power by John White
Joy Unspeakable by Martyn Lloyd-Jones

The Truth Will Set You Free

Satan offers people a guaranteed formula for emotional and spiritual upheaval: *Never use Scripture as a standard of truth, and always keep what you think, feel or believe deeply hidden.* Keeping a person from openness and vulnerability gives the evil one the necessary ground to harass and harm that person's life. Satan uses whatever an individual hides to distort, deceive and eventually destroy him or her. Darkness is his playground, and he will use every hidden thought or wound or false belief to choke the very life from a person. All the while he works to convince people that rejection, scorn and shame await if others find out what is really there. So, to one degree or another, we hide . . . and we lose.

People experiencing seasons of emotional and spiritual upheaval are most often there because of such hiddenness. The Lord wants them free, so He allows the desperation of darkness to settle in as a motivation to bring things into the light. Only in the light can healing begin. True freedom demands that every thought, feeling and belief be open to examination. Though initially painful and potentially frightening, honest unveiling before the Lord is the only way to see wounds healed, distorted thoughts untwisted, false beliefs eliminated and sinful enslavement ended. Satan works in hiding, but Jesus sets people free through truth and honesty.

The principle that "the truth will set you free" (John 8:32) has the potential to transform a person's life. I have repeatedly seen men and women change radically and wonderfully—people who were previously locked up inside—as they bring things into the light. An inexplicable supernatural transaction occurs that is almost visibly observable. These "truth encounters" snatch power away from the evil one and place the essence of life securely into the hands of Jesus Christ. The Lord empowers people to align their thoughts and beliefs with God's Word, and new wholeness replaces the fractured fragments of their old ways of living. The result: ever-increasing freedom.

In our search for freedom we must consider several different aspects of truth. These will be the focus of this chapter. But before we start, it is important that we realize three things about facing truth.

First, most of us have lived a long time hiding certain feelings and thoughts and embracing various false beliefs. Most likely we took these on as children as a way of interpreting or controlling our world. As children we were probably not able to see what was really there or discern the difference between what was deception and what was true.

Therefore—and this is the second point—we need the guidance of the Holy Spirit every step of the way. Paul told us that where the Spirit is, there is freedom (see 2 Corinthians 3:17). We need to surrender to His internal search, submitting to His sanctifying process. The Holy Spirit (as we noted in the last chapter) is our most important Counselor, so we must be sure to turn this entire process over to Him.

Finally, remember that finding freedom is not the result of a single spiritual experience. It comes about through an ongoing encounter with the Holy Spirit. It involves seeing what is hidden and distorted, repenting and releasing all that is not of God, and discovering and embracing the truth that sets people free. This process will be difficult and takes time, but the Lord is there to give encouragement and strength.

Face the Truth about Sin in Your Life

Although talking against sin is unpopular in some churches today, it must be addressed head on. Every attitude, action and appetite of the flesh is ground for Satan's activity. He will use each one to enslave people in self-destructive behavior, shame them with feelings of guilt and self-rejection and separate them from the intimacy God intends. While sin seems pleasing for a season, it ultimately disappoints and destroys. It is serious business—so much so that Jesus gave His life to free people from its death grip.

I am sure you understand that your old nature was crucified with Christ. But many of your sinful ways remain—dark habits of your non-Christian past. You may have embraced these behaviors in order to dull some pain or bring a sense of pleasure. Things like sexual immorality, rage, dishonesty, selfishness or manipulation may have become a way of life. But freedom demands that you count yourself dead to sin and go on to walk according to your new life in Christ Jesus.

Many people come to me for spiritual direction in the midst of trying times. Numerous issues lie behind their problems, but invariably there is sin in their lives that, unaddressed, leaves them little hope for long-term freedom. I encourage them, in an atmosphere of compassion and understanding, to face the truth about the sin in their lives. In each case I seek to guide them to make the following responses to whatever it is God reveals.

Seeing the truth about sin is not enough. You must go on to:

> Recognize and confess each sin before the Lord.
> Repent from evil and turn toward God.
> Renounce any foothold Satan had in this area of your life.
> Receive Christ's promised forgiveness.
> Realign your life according to God's Word through obedience.
> Rejoice in the love and grace of your heavenly Father.

What results are the promised "times of refreshing . . . from the Lord" for your life (Acts 3:19).

Blatant Sin

The first level of sin you must address is that of blatant rebellion. Surrender any and all areas of open and obvious disobedience to Christ if you hope to experience some degree of freedom.

Roger Collins wanted help during a season of trial but was hesitant to talk with me. He knew I would eventually challenge him about the way he treated his wife. I was well aware of his selfish preoccupation with men's softball, which took him away from Doris regularly. Night after night she was left at home as Roger made his way to yet another game. In the summer he was gone over numerous weekends for special tournaments. I had talked with him before, and Roger knew that his commitment to softball was way out of line and costly to his relationship with Doris. He had refused to budge, however, even though he admitted this was selfish.

Roger was rebelling against God and neglecting his responsibilities. Now for several months he had been experiencing emotional upheaval, and finally had come to talk about it. Before Roger walked through the door, he must have known that, sooner or later, I would bring up the matter of his selfishness. And he was right.

The pathway to freedom lies through repentance. Inner peace and open disobedience are in direct dissonance, unable to abide in the same life. If Roger wanted God's *shalom,* he had to face the truth about his sin.

Secret Sin

Second, the Holy Spirit will challenge you to face the truth about any and all secret sin. It is possible to hide certain sinful behaviors from others, but never from God. Sooner or later He will call you to deal with what goes on in the dark and hidden places of your life, which is far too costly to overlook. He demands that it be brought into the light for repentance and restoration.

My son, in his early twenties and a youth intern at an area church, has a growing love for and devotion to the Lord. Generally enthusiastic about life, Aaron went through an extended season of discouragement recently. After some time he came to talk with me about his feelings.

"Dad," he said at one point, "there's something I need to tell you. It's been bothering me for a good while now, but I've been afraid to talk about it. But I can't carry this around anymore."

He went on to confess some behavior in high school that was clearly wrong. Though long past and forgiven by the Lord, it ate at him. Aaron had tried to hold in secret something that needed to be brought into the light. Hidden away, Satan used the past to harass Aaron continually. Bringing the truth into the open brought tremendous freedom to him and great joy to me.

Countless times the Holy Spirit has uncovered secret sin in the lives of people seeking my help. The issues vary, from sexual sin to business fraud. Normally individuals are hesitant to open up, battling shame and fearing rejection. Often this is due to previous experience with a legalistic church or a Christian who reacted punitively. But it is essential that we press through all hesitation, confronting our brokenness by coming clean before the Lord. Hidden sin enslaves and destroys, but God's love brings freedom and life. Paul encouraged his readers to "[renounce] secret and shameful ways" (2 Corinthians 4:2), getting everything out into the Lord's healing light.

Unknown Sin

Third, in facing the truth about sin, you will most likely discover that some of what you thought was acceptable behavior is, in fact, both unbiblical and unhealthy. In opening yourself to the Holy Spirit, you will find that He often reveals sin where you do not see it (and most likely society does not). Countless culturally acceptable mores do not line up with God's Word. Desensitized by the standards of the world, many Christians live with attitudes and behaviors that compromise their freedom and well-being. But once a believer asks to face the truth, the Holy Spirit will unveil each and every inconsistency, no matter how subtle or seemingly innocent.

Consider, for example, the issue of independence. We in the United States pride ourselves on independence, that fortitude of personality that allows us to stand on our own two feet, make it on our own and forge ahead to blaze new trails and conquer problems singlehandedly. We idolize these "lone rangers" and "rebels" who fight evil and right wrong against all odds—strong, solitary heroes and heroines who ride off into the sunset after conquering the bad guys. We even boast of a declaration of our independence as the foundational document of this nation.

Regardless of any and all blessings of independence, it is fundamentally unbiblical and in reality a destructive myth. The Bible prioritizes relationships and interdependence, community and selfless love. No one individual moves out alone, but instead receives and gives support to others as needed. Even our Lord lived in community, and He told His followers that observable *agape* love within the context of shared life is the standard of His love. By loving one another, He said, "all men will know that you are my disciples" (John 13:35).

Independence, as our society models it, is selfish and competitive and enhances painful loneliness. And in truth, heroes seldom accomplish anything alone. While one person may have received all the accolades, countless others made what he or she did possible by their support.

What is my point? That many Christians are greatly influenced by society's ideas of right and wrong behavior, accepting cultural standards as though they were in line with God's Word. Yet often they are not. Examples of this kind of inconsistency are limitless. Acceptable business practices can be unacceptable to God, as can be attitudes about money, sex, honesty, habits, gossip, bitterness, unforgiveness, bigotry, self-centeredness and much more. Add to these issues of gaining self-worth through performance, status, education or income, and maladjusted ways of relating like aggression, codependency, manipulation, people-pleasing and hiding.

Society would ask, "What's the problem?" But the Word of God shows us these to be sinful and destructive attitudes and actions. And on the journey toward freedom, the Holy Spirit will challenge every habit, appetite and behavior that in any way falls short of God's Word. He does this out of love, seeking to eliminate all ground for evil and to empower people to live healthy, whole lives.

Face the Truth about Wounds You Received

Not all our thoughts, feelings and misbeliefs are the result of being born with sinful natures. Many are the product of deep wounds caused by significant people in our lives at times of vulnerability. The wounding, whether physical or emotional, brought great pain. As a result we probably reacted with some bad choices in hopes of killing the pain and protecting ourselves from further harm.

Some people carry the memories of woundings with them every day. No matter how hard they try to forget, the events are as fresh as when they first happened, clearly affecting the way they live. For others the wounds are subconsciously forgotten or minimized. Hidden beneath layers of negative emotions, coping mechanisms and destructive behavior, they are not readily seen as particular problems. But over time the unaddressed hurt festers, causing increased emotional and spiritual upheaval. People may seek help for the debilitating turmoil they may be experiencing. But they must realize that the most important work lies at the old wound that was never properly attended to.

Eliminating the Discomfort

A friend of mine, Jason Murphy, is a highly efficient and well-respected administrator at a small Christian college. He does his work thoroughly and with the utmost professionalism. Jason dresses well, is polite and lives a well-disciplined life. He is particularly effective in organizational management, so his employer continually gives him responsibilities that demand a take-charge kind of leadership. Jason, it seems, has his act together.

When he was on the West Coast for an educational conference, we had the opportunity to spend several days together. One day we talked about my dark night and various lessons I learned as a result. Jason listened with great empathy and caring, but told me he could not really relate. Life was good, he said, and he did not carry any baggage from the past.

I did not want to suggest anything different, but his response did not sit well with me.

The next day we were driving to Lassen National Park when Jason commented, "You know, Terry, there's something I've been praying about lately. I can get really angry in certain situations. I don't let people know how I'm feeling at the time because it's so wrong. I've been asking the Lord to eliminate it from my life, but so far He hasn't answered my prayer."

As Jason said this, he struggled with nervous embarrassment. But in the end he assured me it was really no big deal and that he could handle it.

I challenged Jason to ask the Holy Spirit to reveal what was behind the anger and face whatever truth He exposed. Jason hesitantly agreed. What followed was a Spirit-directed, gentle peeling back of defenses to expose some core issues in Jason's life.

Our conversation began focusing on the anger itself. The Holy Spirit helped Jason identify the specific situations that made him angry most often. There were two dominant and recurring issues. First, Jason grew angry whenever he sensed disorder and had no power to take control. Second, he began to boil whenever he thought people were perceiving him as incapable or failing to do his best. Conversely, Jason admitted he always felt good when he was able to be in charge and when people affirmed his work.

This led us into a conversation about control and appearance. Jason could see that these two issues were critical to his sense of well-being. They had become the basis of his sense of safety, security and self-worth. I told Jason that true peace and identity were found in God alone, and that his substitutes were unhealthy and ultimately destructive.

It was good that we talked about all this. But we still needed to address the core wound or wounds that lay hidden beneath it all. Several days earlier Jason had assured me there were no significant issues from the past. Now the Spirit was revealing hidden wounds, and Jason was about to face some truth that would be painful at first, yet ultimately freeing.

Jason was the oldest of three brothers. His parents had been real "partyers," often inebriated or stoned. They stayed away from home most nights and weekends, and their lifestyle kept the family in virtual poverty. From an early age Jason was responsible to parent not only himself but his brothers, too. If they were to eat, have clean clothes to wear and get to school, Jason had to make it happen. For years he did. In addition, he often had to caretake his dropout parents.

As we talked about this, Jason told me it was really no big deal. He said he actually liked being in charge as a boy, and that he felt it equipped him to be effective in his jobs as an adult. In point of fact, that was true. But beneath the surface lay a serious wound that initially caused a lot of pain. It set Jason in motion to embrace control to cope with his environment and power as a means of experiencing self-worth and pride.

The wound in this case was that of being essentially abandoned by his parents. He was left to handle a chaotic world on his own. The pain was great, so Jason took charge at an early age to eliminate the discomfort. Guess what? It worked. From then on he handled stress and chaos by taking control and putting things in order. Things appeared fine on the outside, even though at the core they were not. His parents were absent, the children were not receiving proper emotional care and support and Jason was taking on responsibility that was not his to bear. Even though it made him feel good about himself, it set Jason up to manage everything and everyone around him for the rest of his life. It became the way he found peace and self-worth.

Once God revealed this truth, Jason saw it all clearly. He decided to receive long-term counseling that would address his emotional turmoil, improper coping mechanisms and false beliefs, and, most importantly, provide inner healing prayer about the core wounding itself. Now he was on the road to freedom.

Whenever a person faces the truth about a wound from the past, healing prayer is necessary. Granted, the emotions of turmoil and false beliefs must be addressed. But if a person eliminates these without seeking healing for the deep wound, he or she may just find some new, unhealthy way to address the inner pain, and the cycle will repeat itself. The Holy Spirit can bring the Lord's healing power into the wounds of the past. In an upcoming chapter I will discuss in more detail how a person can move to experience that touch.

Be Careful

A few words of warning are in order. First, the Holy Spirit must be in charge of the process of revealing wounds. Some counselors reconstruct "memories" of abuse that never happened. Do not own something in your life just because someone else "perceived" that it happened. Only when the Lord reveals a memory should you accept it as true. Caregivers can ask leading questions, but the truth of what really occurred must be revealed to you, so you can face and deal with it before the Lord.

Second, the purpose of addressing wounds is freedom, not license to take on a victim mentality. While recognition of a wounding may initially bring a certain degree of anger, it must never lead to bitterness, resentment or revenge. A person must face the fact of what happened, mourn the loss before the Lord and then, by the power of God, forgive and rise up to a new way of living. Christians are not to be perpetual victims, but reigning victors in Christ Jesus our Lord.

Many of us, in an attempt to handle the past, deny woundings or minimize their effect. The truth is, wounds hurt, and we often manage the pain in very harmful ways. Over time we experience more and more brokenness and emotional upheaval. Freedom is possible only when, with the Holy Spirit's help, we face the truth about woundings and embrace the process of healing the Lord provides for His children. Once healed, a person is more capable of letting go of coping mechanisms and dysfunctional behavior.

Face the Truth about the Lies You Believe

The truth can set a person free. But it is also undeniable that a lie or false belief can keep someone in bondage for as long as he or she embraces it. Many people are controlled by beliefs they were taught at an early age that simply are not true. These lies are creating attitudes and behaviors in their lives that will ultimately destroy them. Some people do not know they are being driven by such false beliefs, although these lies shape most of what they do. Others realize they believe such maxims but are unaware that these are destructive deceptions. It takes the ministry of the Holy Spirit to reveal the truth about any and all false beliefs, freeing people to live according to God's Word.

In a previous book I wrote, *Wounded: How You Can Find Inner Wholeness and Healing in Him* (Christian Publications, 1994), I spent several chapters discussing false beliefs and their devastating effects on our lives. I refer you there for a more detailed treatment than I can bring here. Also, I want to recommend two works of Robert McGee, *The Search for Significance* (Rapha, 1990) and *The Search for Freedom* (Vine, 1995). These books have shaped my own thinking greatly and serve as practical, powerful resources for anyone needing further help. Identifying and renouncing false beliefs is critical to everyone's spiritual and emotional well-being.

God-Given Longings

People are endowed by God with certain basic longings, meant to be a driving force in their pursuit of Him. True satisfaction of these longings comes only as individuals are in relationship with the heavenly Father. We long for:

Fellowship with God
A secure and safe environment
A sense of worth
Being unique and special
Being important
Being loved and to love
Enjoyment
Fulfillment and meaning in life

As Adam and Eve fellowshiped with God, they experienced harmony with Him that became the source of fulfillment for every longing of life. (Humans find this fulfillment through a variety of God's good gifts, but these are only channels. He alone is the source.) God gave Adam and Eve the uniqueness, love, esteem and peace they needed, and it was for them paradise.

Unfortunately, Satan deceived Adam and Eve into believing fulfillment could come apart from the Father. As a result, all humankind fell into brokenness and disharmony with God, separating people from the only One who could truly fulfill their most essential longings.

While the Fall brought alienation from God, it did not eliminate the longings. So it was that Satan began a powerful deception that continues through today, convincing people that there are ways to meet these needs other than in God. Several false beliefs have become accepted throughout our society. These are so convincing that people commit fully to live by them, ultimately discovering their destructive power. From infancy we are bombarded, both subtly and intentionally, with these lies. The messages come from significant people in our lives and from a society alienated from God. The false beliefs also find a breeding ground in the wounds we receive, which ultimately heighten the need for fulfillment, meaning and security.

Robert McGee suggests there are four foundational false beliefs that plague people.[1] He believes they are the basis of much emotional, mental and spiritual upheaval. These lies, which are rooted in sin, feed on unaddressed wounds of the past and keep people from the freedom that can be theirs in Christ Jesus. The four false beliefs are:

1. I must meet certain standards of performance to feel good about myself.

2. I must be approved by certain people to feel good about myself.
3. Those who fail are unworthy of love and deserve to be punished.
4. I am what I am. I cannot change. I am hopeless.

Let's look for a moment at how these beliefs take root in a person's life. Remember that people are born in sin, separated from God. As a result, all basic longings remain unaddressed, sending people on a search for fulfillment. In addition, woundings occur that are very painful, and a person looks for possible relief by embracing behaviors that end up being very destructive.

Like you, I was born with a longing for significance and acceptance. The brokenness of adults in my life, however, left me questioning my importance and uniqueness at an early age. I also learned that doing things well brought the sense of significance I longed for. In addition, it became clear that failure resulted in rejection and emotional distance. All this reinforced the false belief that meeting certain standards of performance brings worth to one's life. The combination of unmet longings, wounds of rejection and a powerful false belief set me on a course of workaholism that eventually led to breakdown.

Freedom from such destructive beliefs involves three steps: first, reconciliation with God through Jesus Christ, reuniting a person with the true Source of everything one needs in life. The second step (as I mentioned in the last section) is identifying and healing previous wounding. And third, renouncing particular false beliefs and replacing them with the truth of God's Word. (We will talk more about this in the next section.) These steps enable a person to turn from all sinful behavior that is grounded in these false beliefs and live as the Lord intended.

Facing the truth about false beliefs is an essential step toward freedom. I am convinced that many Christians live broken lives because of them—and unnecessarily so. Christ Jesus provides believers with "everything we need for life and godliness" (2 Peter 1:3). To all who repent of sin—which is, in fact, seeking fulfillment in ungodly ways—God offers reconciliation and a transformed life. Freedom is possible if we will discover all that is ours in Christ Jesus and walk according to that truth.

The Truth about What Is Ours in Christ Jesus

We all know that the evil one wants to keep men and women, boys and girls from accepting the Lord. But if he fails there, Satan works diligently to keep believers from discovering all that is theirs in Jesus. The riches of Christ are unsearchable and eternal, enabling an individual to live in righteousness, peace and joy. The treasury available to Christians is inexhaustible! Yet most of us remain in bondage because we either do not know or do not believe the truth that sets us free.

What has God provided to those who are in Christ Jesus? Let's begin by looking at this question in relation to the four false beliefs we just discussed.

1. In Christ You Are Significant

First, consider the individual trapped in performance as a means of feeling good about himself or herself. Wanting acceptance, importance and significance, he or she strives to achieve, advance and accomplish in order to fill that void. But the truth is, in Christ we receive a new identity as a wonderful gift of grace. Because of Jesus, we are people of infinite worth, referred to in God's Word as

Chosen	John 15:16
Sanctified (set apart)	John 17:17
Children of God	John 1:12
Temples of God	1 Corinthians 3:16
God's workmanship	Ephesians 2:10
Seated with Christ	Ephesians 2:6
Justified by faith in Christ	Romans 5:1

Christians do not need to perform to feel good about themselves. Christ has done it all on the cross, giving us at His expense what we could never buy or earn. Individuals previously bound by performance can stand and declare the truth of their new, Christlike identities. Now they feel significance because of being in Christ, not because of work or achievement. They are now free to serve the Lord as a response to His love, not as a means of feeling worth.

2. In Christ You Are Loved and Accepted

Second, as we have seen, many people are trapped in the hopeless bog of people-pleasing, trying to be accepted and loved by gaining everyone's approval. Such individuals wear themselves out meeting other people's needs in order to please, and they compromise their own agenda and desires in the process. Like performance, people-pleasing is a never-ending and ultimately unsatisfying trap.

But Christ Jesus has once again provided the answer. On the cross He reconciled us to God once and for all. Believers can rest assured that they will never again be rejected by Him. By Jesus' blood we "who once were far away have been brought near" (Ephesians 2:13). His love and acceptance are secure and eternal, capable of meeting every longing we might have for a secure relationship. The truth of God's Word says that believers are

Dearly loved	Ephesians 3:17–19
Reunited with God	1 Corinthians 6:17
Secure in Him and His love	Romans 8:35
Sealed by the Holy Spirit	Ephesians 1:13
Given direct access to God through prayer	Hebrews 10:22
Members of the Lord's Body	1 Corinthians 12:12–31
Owned by the Lord	1 Corinthians 6:19–20

While we still desire relationships with other people, Christians need not be driven to please in order to feel acceptance. Jesus has provided the way for our eternal acceptance. This truth can bring honesty and integrity to former people-pleasers, freeing them to live healthy and balanced lives. Renouncing the false belief that they need approval to feel good about themselves, believers can rest secure in the arms of God's loving embrace.

3. Full Payment Has Been Made

The third false belief involves the fear of failure. Many are trapped in the lie that failing makes one unlovable and deserving of punishment. Like all other false beliefs, this is rooted in sin and reinforced by early childhood experience. At some time this person failed and was rejected or punished as a result. The emotional distance left him or her feeling unworthy and unlovable. Once this lie gets a foothold in a person's life, it can lead to several destructive responses. Some people become perfectionists. Others avoid anything new or risky. Still others, anticipating punishment because of failure, give in to self-abuse or emotional withdrawal. Whatever the response, it enslaves and destroys people.

Once again the Christian comes face to face with God's Word. His truth exposes this lie and releases people from the fear of rejection and punishment. The truth is, Jesus has taken on the full punishment for our sinful failures. On Calvary He received all the rejection and wrath God should have placed on us.

Failure does not mean we are unlovable or deserving of punishment. It simply means we are weak and in need of God's constant help and direction. God's Word tells us that in Christ,

We have been completely forgiven	Ephesians 1:7
Full payment has been made	Colossians 1:13–14
There is no condemnation	Romans 8:1
Cleansing has been accomplished	Hebrews 10:22
We have been given eternal life	Romans 6:23
We have been made complete	Colossians 2:10

4. You Are a New Creature

Many people feel permanently defective, hopelessly unable to change. This is the fourth false belief from which the truth sets us free.

Stacy, by all appearances, was an attractive, successful member of our congregation. She was knowledgeable in Scripture and sought after as a Bible teacher. She also was managing a deep, horrible wound. Her father had sexually violated her repeatedly while Stacy was a teenager. This brought tremendous shame and self-rejection, masked by a well-ordered defense structure. Stacy needed inner healing prayer regarding the wounding, but she also had to know and believe the truth that Christ had changed her. She was not permanently defective and hopeless. In Christ Jesus Stacy had been made new.

People struggling with shame need to understand the truth about Christ's work at the cross. There He bore all our shame, and by His wounds He makes it possible for us to be whole. This work is called regeneration, and it has the power to shatter false belief number four. Numerous Scriptures affirm this truth:

We are new creations in Christ Jesus	2 Corinthians 5:17
By His wounds we are healed	Isaiah 53:5
He will complete the work He began	Philippians 1:6
We are His workmanship	Ephesians 2:10
We are newly born of imperishable seed	1 Peter 1:23
We have been made perfect	Hebrews 10:14
Though once dead in sin, we are now alive in Christ Jesus	Ephesians 2:4–5

Whenever the evil one presses in to make a person hide or feel worthless, he or she can boldly declare the truth of God's transforming work at the cross.

If you are struggling with sin that enslaves, wounds that cripple or lies that destroy, I know a way of healing and deliverance. Allow the Holy Spirit access to your life. He will point out all truth to you and the truth will set you free.

For Further Reading

The Search for Significance by Robert S. McGee
The Search for Freedom by Robert S. McGee
The Bondage Breaker by Neil Anderson
Wounded: How You Can Find Wholeness and Inner Healing through Him by Terry Wardle
The Renewal of the Mind by John and Loren Sandford

5

Forgetting Your Past May Not Be Enough

My parents hosted a tremendous party on their fiftieth wedding anniversary. Friends and family members traveled from across the country, many seeing each other for the first time in decades. It was a wonderful time to tell stories from the past and review old friendships. I thoroughly enjoyed the celebration, particularly watching my mom and dad move among the tables in obvious delight.

At one point in the evening my sister and I were sitting at a table talking with several relatives. During the course of the conversation, we all began to reminisce about our grandmother. Granny, as she insisted we call her, had been a delightful lady who left every grandchild with happy memories. My sister, the oldest of all the grandchildren, was especially close to Granny. Even our conversation at the table touched a bittersweet sorrow in Bonny. It had been nearly a decade since Granny's homegoing, but my sister still felt the pain of her passing.

Bonny began to open up a bit and commented about how difficult it was seeing Granny's home sold recently. She and Grandpap had lived in the white two-story by the train tracks for more than half a century. Bonny said it bothered her to think that someone outside the family now owned Granny's house.

As she said that, I, too, felt a sense of loss and disappointment. Many things had happened in that house that shaped my life. Seeing it go was hard, even though it was perfectly reasonable and right under the circumstances.

But as soon as Bonny made the comment about her feelings, one of our relatives shot back, "Bonny, it's all in the past. Forget it. It's over!"

For a moment you could have cut the silence with a knife. It was obvious to me that the issue touched more hearts around that table than my sister's. But for that family member, the solution to the past was somehow to erase it all and move on.

But it is just not that easy. Like it or not, much of who we are and how we feel, act and respond in life is shaped by the past. Things we experienced, heard or thought have made a significant impression on our lives. The past affects the present continually because it establishes a pattern of interpretation and behavioral response to everyday events. Much of what took place in the past has left a positive and useful endowment for our lives. But some things in our personal histories have programmed us for serious problems.

You and I experienced things that were harmful to our well-being. In some cases it was unbiblical advice about how to react to certain situations, or value judgments on what is important in life. At times we were hurt, betrayed, abused or abandoned by important people in our lives. Previous choices also mark our past that were clearly out of God's will. These events often affect our attitudes, actions and appetites in the present moment.

Saying, "Just forget the past" does not automatically erase the effects that previous experiences have on us. Untended wounds still cause us pain. Previous betrayals make us critically cautious. Sin unrepented of keeps us from freedom. Unhealthy behavior patterns continue to enslave. You can possibly forget the *what* and *when* of past events, but it takes more than forgetting to free you from negative patterns that the past has shaped in your life.

Let me suggest three steps. First, find freedom from the past by identifying any and all problematic feelings, behaviors, reactions and bondages that are influencing your life negatively. For example, do you have unreasonable fears, jealousy, anger or despair? Are there any consistently negative behaviors wearing you down, like performance or people-pleasing? Do you react inappropriately in certain situations or with a particular kind of person? Have you struggled continually with some area of sin and cannot seem to move on to freedom? Remember, if asked, the Holy Spirit will help you identify the problems that compromise your spiritual well-being and maturity.

Second, once these patterns or problems are identified, ask the Lord to reveal where and when they started. They are rooted somewhere in the past, so instead of forgetting previous events, prayerfully press in to them. An example might be your attitude toward educated people. Maybe you feel uncomfortable or resentful around them and consistently back away in silence. You may think you always felt this way, but the truth is, some event or instruction from your past set this pattern in motion. It was either caught or taught in an earlier encounter. In each case, the problems and patterns must be linked before freedom from the past can truly be experienced.

Third, move to either undo, relearn, receive healing or experience release from the past that caused the patterns or problems you presently face. The precise approach to this varies, depending on the character of the negative event itself. But in each case it is the power of the Lord that works to free you, so the context of prayer and faith is always essential to the process. It is also important to work through the issues in a supportive environment of spiritually mature friends, family members or caregivers.

Problems and negative patterns of your life signal the places you need God to work. The journey through the dark night will certainly take you to these issues, but it is your decision whether to allow Him to address them or not. Pressing in to the past with the Lord is painful, yet ultimately freeing. He releases you from the chains that bind you to attitudes, behaviors and reactions clearly inconsistent with spiritual health and well-being. To ignore, deny or try to forget may make you feel better initially, but it keeps you entangled in the destructive events of your past.

In this chapter we will look at four specific ways we can give attention to our past and release the Holy Spirit's powerful ministry.

Healing the Wounds of Your Past

Julie came to my wife, Cheryl, and me for help because of the chronic anger and resentment she was pouring out on her children. She felt unreasonably intolerant of their normally rambunctious behavior, she said, and her reactions were often verbally abusive, filled at times with shaming and demeaning remarks. Julie knew she needed help and was willing to do whatever it took to change her behavior. A devoted believer, she wanted to move beyond any destructive patterns of her past.

We asked Julie if she would allow the Holy Spirit to reveal the root issues beneath this problem. She agreed. So through numerous meetings, we worked through the events that the Spirit exposed.

Most importantly we discovered that Julie had been raised by a rage-filled, performance-dominated father.

His actions had repeatedly wounded Julie as a child, leaving her with unresolved emotional conflict and confusion. These unhealed wounds still hurt deep inside, causing her to struggle with feelings of inferiority, guilt and shame. She had also adopted a behavior pattern similar to her father's. Julie needed help, and the solution began with inner healing prayer.

Let me pause for a moment to define what I mean by the phrase *inner healing prayer*. It represents an activity of the Holy Spirit founded on the work of Christ on Calvary. The focus of the Spirit's ministry involves identifying the root woundings that cause emotional upheaval and problem behavior. Then, using prayer as the foundation, the Holy Spirit brings healing to the painful memories and deliverance from the strongholds of sin. This inner healing is possible because Jesus Christ was victorious over all forms of brokenness and sin. It is available to every person who turns to Him in openness and humility.

Countless people stay trapped, I believe, because of improper reactions to the wounds of the past. Inner healing prayer offers us a pathway to freedom and well-being.

It may be helpful to walk through inner healing prayer as it took place in Julie's life. Her problems resemble many of our own issues. The pathway she took for healing is available to us all. We need only recognize the symptoms of wounding in our lives, such as emotional turmoil or destructive behavior. Once these are identified, we must turn to the Lord for healing and release.

Our meetings with Julie began with a season of praise. Then I invited the Holy Spirit to guide us, and I prayed on the armor of God, according to Ephesians 6:10–18, for each of us. Cheryl and I asked the Holy Spirit to surface the particular event He wanted to work on in Julie's life for that day. We asked Julie to trust in the Spirit's involvement and share the details of the experience He brought to mind. But first, before she began to recount a specific experience, Cheryl and I asked the Lord to bring back to her memory everything necessary for healing. Our style was conversational, moving in and out of prayer as appropriate.

At one point Julie began to tell us about a very painful memory. It involved her father raging over what he perceived to be a violation of a clear family rule. He stormed at Julie in a public setting, spanked her abusively, then made numerous shaming statements. The ugly irony in this case is that his perception was wrong. She had not violated the rule, but her pleas to explain went unheeded.

After Julie detailed this abusive event, we asked the Holy Spirit to release the pent-up emotion. We instructed Julie to imagine that her father was there, and to tell him how she felt and the impact this experience had had on her. Immediately rage began to pour out. She spoke of the unfairness of the punishment and her frustration at not being heard. She talked about how this abuse and shaming made her feel. Words like *humiliated, violated, worthless, rejected* and *insecure* were mentioned. She also verbalized feelings of isolation, since her father had distanced himself from her emotionally as part of her ongoing punishment and as a shaming period aimed at changing her behavior.

Throughout this unleashing Cheryl and I prayed and encouraged Julie that she was safe. We expressed the compassion and love of God toward her, assuring Julie that He was right there with us.

Once she had fully expressed her pain and emotion, our prayers shifted. Cheryl and I asked the Lord Jesus to enter the memory with Julie. We encouraged her to surrender her imagination and mental vision to the Lord as instruments of healing. (Dr. David Seamands, in his book *Healing Damaged Emotions,* refers to this as "sanctified imagination.") As the Spirit led, we spoke the truth

97

of God's Word into the situation. Julie imagined Jesus comforting her as she wept following her abuse. Cheryl and I spoke specific Scriptures and truths expressing Christ's love, acceptance and compassion. We focused in particular on her new identity in Christ—her worth, uniqueness and belonging. I asked the Holy Spirit to touch her wounds and assure her of her healing and right standing before God.

Then, continuing in the atmosphere of prayer, we moved at the Spirit's leading to two important actions. First, we encouraged Julie to see her father through the eyes of Jesus and then to express forgiveness. This involved a significant period of waiting. But the Spirit led gently and faithfully, empowering her to say, "Daddy, I forgive you." Second, we led her in prayer, renouncing any foothold Satan had in her life through this event. Finally we closed by thanking the Lord for His deep work and sealing all that had happened by the power of the Holy Spirit.

The process took time, but after numerous sessions, Cheryl and I watched Julie move to new freedom and increased spiritual vitality. By addressing the wounds of her past, Julie was able to move beyond it to a brighter future in Christ.[1]

Freedom from Bitter Root Judgments

Gloria Reese, sitting in the back of one of my undergraduate theology classes, made it clear that she did not like me. No matter what I did, she answered my questions abruptly, avoided any casual conversation and took exception with what I said whenever the opportunity presented itself. Over the course of the semester just about everyone in the class picked up on her feelings toward me. The tension was so obvious that it made the situation uncomfortable. I tried everything—encouragement, affirmation, compliments, concern—all to no avail.

One day I found myself face to face with Gloria at the local mall. I decided to address the issue head on. I asked her for a moment of her time and said, "Gloria, it is obvious that you have a problem with me. But frankly, I don't know why. Have I done something to hurt or offend you? If so, would you tell me what it was, because I want to make it right with you."

I saw a noticeable change in her countenance. She seemed to soften and tears welled up in her eyes.

"Dr. Wardle, I guess it really isn't about you," she said after a pause. "I just don't like being in your class. I feel very uncomfortable there, like you're going to embarrass me or something."

"Have I done that to you?" I asked. "Or have you heard that I've done it with someone else?"

No, she said, but she went on to explain that a male high school teacher had humiliated her once in a class. He had ridiculed her work and everyone ended up laughing at her. Then Gloria told me I reminded her of him, so she was protecting herself through an angry, resentful attitude.

Gloria was making what John Sandford calls a "bitter root judgment" against me. An unresolved conflict in her past had preconditioned a negative attitude and response to any situation or person in any way similar. It was a sinful and destructive pattern that was affecting me, the other students and Gloria herself. Her only hope for freedom was dealing with the past event so it would stop infesting the present.

Every one of us suffers from bitter root judgments. This is the second part from the past from which we can find release through the Holy Spirit's ministry. A bad situation may have programmed you to react negatively in similar circumstances. The range of possibilities is endless. An unpleasant experience with a boss, parent, teacher or pastor may have hurt you deeply. A seed of resentment was planted in your life, so that now all authority figures must eat the bitter fruit of your reaction. You dislike or mistrust them all simply because they are in leadership. Your attitude and behavior have nothing to do with their actions or character. You are superimposing your judgment from the past on the present.

The writer of Hebrews warned Christians about such behavior. He wrote,

> Make every effort to live in peace with all men and to be holy; without holiness no one will see the Lord. See to it that no one misses the grace of God and that no bitter root grows up to cause trouble and defile many.
>
> Hebrews 12:14–15

Using the example of Gloria, you can easily see how many ways such judgments are out of line with God's Word. First, she was not "[living] in peace with all men" because she held unresolved resentment in her heart about the situation in high school. Second, she was missing the grace of God in that she had not extended forgiveness, based on the Lord's forgiveness of her. Third, she had allowed the bitter root toward male teachers to "[grow] up to cause trouble." And her reactions were defiling people each time she acted on her past judgment.

What is true of Gloria is equally true of you in the areas of your bitter roots. Such attitudes and patterns of behavior are clearly wrong and need to be addressed before the Lord.

Once you identify areas in which you have bitter root judgments, allow the Holy Spirit access to your life to rid you of them. Bitter roots keep you from freedom and spiritual well-being. I suggest the following steps.

First, seek the Lord's healing for the original wound you received. (This process was outlined in the previous section of this chapter.) Second, confess and repent of the resentment, bitterness and anger you have been holding against anyone involved. While it may have been a way to protect yourself or seek revenge, such attitudes are wrong. They are sin. Third, extend forgiveness to the person or persons who wounded you. Granted, this is not easy, but it is a necessary requirement of the Kingdom. Jesus forgave you, and you in turn must forgive those who hurt you. (We will say much more about this in chapter 7.) Finally, stop the reactive behavior. When you find yourself in a similar circumstance and your emotions kick in automatically, stop and say to yourself, *Am I responding to the present or reacting out of the past? Is this circumstance or person engaging old feelings because of similarity to my previous experience? I need to respond to the present as Christ would have me, not out of past bitter root judgments.*

Working through this issue will bring you incredible peace and spiritual vitality. It will open the door to a much better future, free from the defiling enslavements of the past. I recommend *Transformation of the Inner Man* by John and Paula Sandford for more on this subject. Their teaching on bitter roots—the best material available on the topic—is insightful, thoroughly biblical and practical in its application.

Freedom from What We Learned

Not all your false beliefs and negative behaviors are the result of past wounding or bad experiences. Much of what you believe or do—this is the third way you can find healing from the past—is simply a result of what you learned early in life. Either someone taught you that such attitudes and behaviors were the right way to respond, or you gave them a try, found they worked and have reacted that way ever since.

What We Have Been Taught

Bob Lewis knelt at the altar crying after the visiting missionary extended the invitation for people to give their lives to cross-cultural ministry. Ever since becoming a Christian, Bob had wanted to serve the Lord in full-time Christian service. But every time he really considered making the commitment, he came up against one insurmountable obstacle: money.

It wasn't that Bob was greedy. He and his wife gave generously to the church and to missionary support. But Bob knew that serving the Lord as a missionary would reduce his income radically and demand daily dependence on the Lord. Such a decision is difficult for anyone, but for Bob it was the major obstacle to following the Lord's calling.

Bob asked to talk to me about this matter, so we scheduled several lunchtime meetings. I began by asking him questions about his past that might unlock this bondage. I was interested to see if he had been raised in poverty or had gone through a personal financial crisis. No, there had been no wound or bad experience behind his attitude about money.

I did learn, though, that Bob's parents had put great emphasis on financial responsibility and security. His dad had taught him early in life the value of earning and saving money. Over the years Bob's parents had emphasized that money brought security and enabled a person to provide for his family. In fact, this was a central principle of his parents' philosophy of life, which had in turn forged his own beliefs.

Unfortunately, what Bob had learned was inconsistent with Scripture. It teaches that God and God alone is our source of provision and security, and that He promises to meet our needs as we focus on His Kingdom. And because Bob's attitudes about money did not match up with Scripture, he was opening the door for Satan to enslave him in a false belief.

You and I often respond to life situations based on attitudes and value judgments we learned as children that are not at all biblical. We embraced these precepts, modeled or taught by significant adults in our lives, as truth, and built highly developed patterns of behavior on deceptive structures. Satan uses these as places to harass and enslave our lives.

Often we are not even aware of how seriously false beliefs are affecting our spiritual health and development. Virtually every area of belief and behavior is susceptible to such deception. Much of what you and I believe about ourselves, God, others, marriage, work, sexuality, morals and ethics was shaped by other people's beliefs. Attitudes about the poor, the mentally ill, the handicapped or the racially diverse were determined early in our lives as we listened to and watched the adults in our world. If what they taught contradicted Scripture, it may have become a seedbed for serious problems in adulthood.

It does not take a wound or bad experience. All we need is embracing an unbiblical attitude, behavior or value judgment early in life in order to invite the bondage of the evil one into our future.

What We Think Has Worked

In some cases, what we believe or do today was not taught by someone else. We learned the behavior in childhood and stayed committed to it (perhaps unconsciously) because we believe it works.

Tom Evans is generally an amiable, polite fellow. That is, until he does not get what he wants. Then he reacts in rage or in a royal pity party. It is one of the most childlike displays you will ever see—a 41-year-old man acting like a five-year-old, throwing a major temper tantrum to get his way.

Tom adopted that behavior in early childhood and never abandoned it. Subconsciously he believes it works, so he engages in the destructive pattern whenever necessary. Most people give in to it because it is so embarrassingly ugly. His actions also give clear evidence that the enemy now uses that practice to hurt Tom and slime everyone around when he does it.

There are countless ways that negative behavior shows up in our lives. Our reactions to perceived danger, rejection, chaos, abandonment, punishment and failure are often patterns learned in childhood. The reactions seem branded into our lives so deeply that we cannot do otherwise. The truth is that, unchallenged, these reactions and behaviors are the very places where the evil one controls our lives. He uses them as stumblingblocks to our spiritual growth, obstacles preventing wholeness and maturity. As we journey through seasons of trial and difficulty, these are the places where the enemy will most likely hang us up. As such, we must take this ground away from him and align our lives with the Word of God.

Breaking Free

As with everything we have been discussing, freedom is yours in Christ Jesus. He has the power to release you from all deceptive ways, false beliefs and unbiblical reactions. While the journey to wholeness takes time, progress is assured as you surrender to the Lord's work in your life.

Freedom from destructive beliefs and responses learned in childhood involves several key steps. Once again, you must identify any false beliefs and behaviors in your life. This is a work of the Holy Spirit initiated by Him at your request. He will reveal every inconsistency, be it through God's Word, counsel, prayer or circumstances. His light will shine on the negative issues of your past so you will know clearly where the problems are.

Second, repent of these beliefs and behaviors, renouncing any and all influence the evil one may have held in your life in these areas. Claiming your victory in Christ, you can command him and any of his evil cohorts to leave you alone.

Third, learn and embrace God's truth as the standard of your behavior and responses to life situations. Scripture is your rule in all matters of faith and practice. You must replace what you learned with the precepts of Kingdom life, praying that the Holy Spirit will empower you to walk accordingly. This means you need to choose consciously to respond differently from your previous, childlike patterns. Tom must set aside temper tantrums as a means of controlling others. He must obey the guidance of Scripture, which prioritizes a servant approach to relationships. As you choose new, biblical patterns of behavior, the evil one is no longer able to hold you in bondage. Instead, the Holy Spirit will enable you to move on to a new level of spiritual vitality and maturity.

I want to close this section with the words of Paul: "When I was a child, I talked like a child, I thought like a child, I reasoned like a child. When I became a man, I put childish ways behind me" (1 Corinthians 13:11). It is time for many of us to follow this admonition.

Freedom from Unresolved Relational Issues

In the Sermon on the Mount, Jesus emphasized the critical relationship between intimacy with the heavenly Father and harmony among His children. Matthew recorded the words of Christ:

> "If you are offering your gift at the altar and there remember that your brother has something against you, leave your gift there in front of the altar. First go and be reconciled to your brother; then come and offer your gift."
>
> Matthew 5:23–24

I believe Jesus is telling us that to open the channel between us and God, we must be willing to clear up any obstacles between us and other people. This is the fourth way we can attend to our past and release the Holy Spirit's powerful ministry. Relational dissonance makes it hard to hear the whispers of God. Anyone desiring to grow close to Him must right the unresolved issues of the past. Forgetting what happened is not enough. We must do our part in correcting genuine problems and reconciling with our brothers or sisters.

Life together on this planet is not an easy proposition. The history of wars and statistics about murder, abuse and divorce make that point all too obvious. But in a world of hatred and disharmony, Christians are called to live together in love (see John 13:34). We are to be witnesses of true Kingdom life; to encourage, support and care for one another, as well as extend patience, understanding and forgiveness. In an atmosphere dominated by grace, believers are to live according to the pattern of 1 Corinthians 13. Paraphrasing the words of Paul, we are to be patient and kind, avoiding all envy, boasting, pride and rudeness. We are to care for others more than ourselves; to be patient and forgiving; to be repulsed by evil and joyful in the truth. Believers should protect one another with perceptive trust and hope. And no matter what, we should never give up on each other, because we are family—God's family.

But the truth is, we do not always act this way. Conflicts arise that cause tension, disappointments and misunderstanding. We hurt people's feelings and do things at times that are terribly selfish and destructive. While we have been made new in Christ, a lot of our old behavior still dominates the way we relate to one another. Too often we fail to resolve our conflicts, moving on in life without adequate reconciliation and in some cases restoration. Harsh words, misunderstandings, gossip or hurtful actions cause hard feelings. Distance often results between people, and we develop feelings of resentment or ill ease.

Sometimes our solution is simply to avoid those people and move on into the future. When we do, however, the unresolved issues become obstacles to our spiritual growth and a seedbed for the enemy's work. We must resolve our part in these conflicts, no matter how large or small. Even if the other party resists our efforts, we must do whatever we can to lay a foundation for reconciliation.

Raymond Helsing became a Christian in middle age. As a secular entrepreneur, he had stepped on a lot of people climbing the ladder of success. He had made a great deal of money, but also plenty of enemies. Many people used or cheated by Raymond stayed as far away from him as possible.

When Raymond became a Christian, he took the reconciliation teaching of Jesus to heart. He contacted every person the Holy Spirit brought to mind, confessed his sinful behavior and asked forgiveness. Many people were, to say the least, shocked. Others, locked in bitterness, refused to be reconciled with him. Some individuals adopted a wait-and-watch attitude. But Raymond was also committed to restore any money he had received unfairly. People he had cheated were repaid in full, and standing debts were cleared.

Raymond was removing obstacles along the path to spiritual maturity. Reconciliation and restoration not only brought renewed relationships to Raymond; they helped him defeat the evil one and unleash new life in the Holy Spirit.

You cannot just move on into the future without addressing what is left undone in the past. You can move beyond your painful past and on to incredible freedom and spiritual growth. But not before you address the wounds, bitter roots, negative behavior patterns and unresolved relationships that are still affecting your life. The journey through difficult times brings these matters right to the surface. In truth, this is an act of the Father's grace, painful as it may be. For there, right before you, the issues are brought to plain sight demanding your serious attention. Led and empowered by the Holy Spirit, you can be set free, healed, renewed and reconciled for new life—if only you surrender to the process.

Granted, it takes time and often help from other Christians. But if you ask, the Lord will reveal where you need reconciliation and restoration. According to Jesus, God will most likely bring situations to mind as you press in to know Him better. There, before His throne, the Lord will show you whom to approach and what to do. Reconciliation will most likely involve dialogue, explanation, confession and forgiveness. At times you will need to take practical steps toward restoration by making right any and all wrongs you have committed.

Is it risky? Of course! But it is far more hazardous to allow the unresolved issues to remain. The journey toward freedom demands that you move ahead by taking the steps to right your past. Because in the end, closing the door to the past is a giant step toward a new beginning.

Further Reading

Transformation of the Inner Man by John and Paula Sandford
Healing of Memories by David Seamands
Putting Away Childish Things by David Seamands
Healing Woman's Emotions by Paula Sandford
Healing Life's Hidden Addictions by Archibald Hart

6

Feelings Tell You More Than You Think

The journey through difficulty often generates emotional upheaval. Experience tells me there is a right and wrong way to handle it. If we respond correctly, our feelings can lead us to greater wholeness and enhance spiritual growth. But if we react to our emotions or ignore what they are trying to tell us, we invite ongoing pain and ultimately disaster. We must recognize that spiritual development is undeniably linked to emotional well-being.

Yet reacting automatically to emotional upheaval or ignoring our feelings altogether comes more naturally than responding properly and maturely. Some individuals act on everything they feel without consideration or restraint. Their motto is "If it feels good, do it." So they let go with harmful behaviors driven by fear, anger, bitterness or any one of countless other emotions. They leave destruction in their wake, and in the end nothing is better, nothing is solved.

I have a friend who wears his feelings right out front. If he feels it, you know it. He seldom stops to consider what lies behind his emotional upheaval, other than blaming the crisis of the moment. The truth is, he has plenty of unresolved issues and false beliefs that keep him in a perpetual emotional stew. But he does not take the time to listen; he simply reacts. It is hard to handle his emotional barrages, but when confronted he says, "I was just being honest." That is not true, because he has never stopped to see what lies at the base of the upheaval. He acts on feelings but does not give himself permission to touch the real upheaval deep inside. Frankly, he is toxic to himself and everyone around him, in spiritual bondage and unable to move to the peace that Jesus has for him. He is stuck.

My reaction to feelings was exactly the opposite. I worked hard to shut them down whenever possible, particularly when they were negative. Somewhere along the line I embraced the false idea that it was wrong to have bad feelings. I thought they meant I was not as good a Christian as I should be. So, wanting to be perceived as spiritual, I learned to shut down. On one occasion someone said something against me in a public forum and a colleague asked if I was upset. "Not at all," I told him. "I put the matter in the Lord's hands." It sounded noble, but I was being dishonest with myself and my friend. I had "stuffed" my emotions so fast I did not even have time to know what I was feeling.

For years I approached my emotions like this. In fact, my staff remarked repeatedly on my ability to remain poker-faced in a tough situation. I took pride in the "gift," even recommending it as a worthy goal on the path to spiritual maturity. The truth is, I was setting myself up for a major breakdown. Years of stuffed feelings were accumulating inside, looking for the opportunity to get out.

As the stress of responsibility grew, my ability to remain in control weakened. Toward the end, right before entering my dark night, this weakening control resulted in unreasonable outbursts of fear, weeping and anger over the slightest problem. Even then I did not listen to what my emotions were trying to tell me. They were serving as an alarm, signaling problems inside and destructive false beliefs. My reaction was simply to turn off the alarm. Failure to pay attention and express my feelings before God led to a serious breakdown and deep spiritual conflict. It has taken several years to unclog the mess of my past and sort out all that my feelings were trying to tell me. Now I am committed to expressing my feelings in a safe spiritual environment in order to listen and respond appropriately.

Be assured I am not at all advocating basing decisions or actions on emotions. I am, on the other hand, urging you not to ignore your feelings. Failing to understand and express your emotions properly can lead to serious problems. Most often you will find yourself making unhealthy attempts at eliminating or silencing their constant cry. In doing so you fail to address the real issues that are the seedbed of the upheaval inside you. You can also invite greater spiritual bondage by stuffing and denying what you are really feeling.

What God's Word Teaches Us

Jesus did not suppress His feelings. Over and again in Scripture we read that He responded emotionally to the events of His life, with not only positive but negative emotions as well. Consider the following passages (emphasis added), which make it plain that our Lord expressed His feelings freely and in a healthy way:

> Filled with *compassion,* Jesus reached out his hand and touched the man.
>
> Mark 1:41

> He looked around at them in *anger* and, deeply *distressed* at their stubborn hearts, said. . . .
>
> Mark 3:5

He was *amazed* at their lack of faith.

Mark 6:6

When Jesus saw this, he was *indignant.*

Mark 10:14

At that time Jesus, full of *joy* through the Holy Spirit, said. . . .

Luke 10:21

. . . He was deeply moved in spirit and *troubled.* "Where have you laid him?" he asked. "Come and see, Lord," they replied. Jesus *wept.*

John 11:33–35

"Love each other as I have *loved* you."

John 15:12

At the ninth hour Jesus cried out in a loud voice, *"Eloi, Eloi, lama sabachthani?"*—which means, "My God, my God, why have you *forsaken* me?"

Mark 15:34

Joy, love, compassion, anger, distress, indignation, amazement and rejection! Jesus did not deny or stuff His feelings at all. Instead He expressed His emotions openly, showing us that, in the right context and in the proper way, it is healthy to let out our true feelings. Any notion that emotions have nothing to do with matters of faith is both dangerous and ridiculous.

Probably the clearest example from the life of Jesus comes from His Gethsemane experience. Facing betrayal and death, Jesus approached God in prayer. Surrounded by a few close friends—clueless friends, I might add—He opened up before His heavenly Father. The Lord wept in distress over the impending mockery, abuse and savage crucifixion. He expressed His apprehensions before God, pouring out His deepest and most disturbing feelings.

As Jesus unlocked the agony of emotional and spiritual turmoil, He aligned Himself perfectly with God's will. He did not hide His true feelings behind pious theological language. Jesus told the Father exactly how He felt, freely expressing the upheaval within. This was key, I believe, to Jesus' moving to the cross in peace, even extending forgiveness without bitterness or resentment to those who crucified Him.

How often Christians attempt to say and do the right thing before dealing with their feelings properly! It is a commonplace approach to spiritual living that ends up doing far more harm than good. Emotions must be reckoned with along the way to well-being. Jesus did, and His example offers a model that we do well to follow.

We learn from Jesus, first, to find a safe context free from condemnation and judgment. Most of us need help in learning to identify and express our deepest emotions. I spend time regularly with my wife or a few close friends, talking through my feelings about situations in my life. It does me no good to pretend all is fine when it is not. If hurt or angry, I get it all out into the light of their godly counsel. I try to discern precisely what I am feeling, and by the Spirit's help how to respond properly. My initial reactions, I know, are most likely out of line with God's will for the moment. Trusted friends and family help me move away from reaction to healthy response.

Let me reemphasize that the environment must be safe. Two things will make the context for sharing your feelings problematic. It is harmful if people move quickly to try to resolve your feelings. How many times have I seen individuals push weeping, hurting people past their emotions to doing the "right" thing! Safety means that supportive people will be patient. The context can also be unsafe if the people around you have a personal investment in the situation or are not working on their own issues. I have a friend who cannot share feelings with her spouse because of the quick reaction of defense. This has virtually shut my friend down from being open and vulnerable. Openness in this case leads to insensitivity and further wounding. "Safe" people are able to empathize, yet not react out of their subjective involvement.

As the second step in handling emotion, take your situation before the Lord in prayer and express your feelings and concerns openly. For a long time I was dishonest with God about my emotional upheaval, fearing His disappointment or disapproval. How wrong I was! You must grow to trust God with your feelings, talking out your concerns before Him. He already knows what is in your heart and why. Opening up before the Lord helps you let out the emotional storm, as well as discover where your thinking is out of line with His truth. (We will talk more about this later in this chapter.)

Third, you must eventually let go of your own desires in the matter and rise up to do the Father's will. I remember feeling angry and hurt by a friend's betrayal. In truth I wanted him to pay, and no matter how hard I tried to pretend otherwise, my feelings were negative and vengeful. I shared the situation with my wife, venting what was deep inside. She listened patiently, loved me and led me to the Father in prayer. I cried out before Him regarding the great harm this situation had brought me, and I did not mince words about my feelings. I told God exactly how hurt and angry the betrayal made me, pouring out bitterness and resentment at the unfairness of it all. But in His presence I began to feel love, understanding and acceptance. I also began to see the depravity of my own heart, which helped me feel less judgmental of my friend. Finally I sensed the Lord calling me to bless and love my friend in spite of his actions.

By God's grace I felt empowered to rise up and do what He wanted, freer and more spiritually refreshed.

Insights from the Psalms

Several years ago I began to use the book of Psalms as part of my own spiritual formation. Each day I spend time reading and praying through one or more of the psalms, meditating on the powerful truths they offer us. I was excited to discover that the psalmists did not hold back their feelings before the Lord. In the context of worship, praise and adoration, they expressed powerful and precise emotions. Initially I was taken aback by their freedom, wondering if they were not pushing it a bit with God. What I learned was that He actually invites such honesty as a way to reveal and deal with our hearts. Feelings can tell a person a great deal about the condition of his or her faith and trust in the sovereign care of God.

Read the Psalms and find people expressing every emotion known to humankind. They are incredible songs filled with love, joy, wonder, awe, delight, amazement, thankfulness and peace. The psalmists wrote verses of truth that exude positive, uplifting and inspiring feelings. Read them prayerfully and find your own heart ignited with passion for the God who is good and full of compassion.

The psalmists equally unleashed the darker feelings that oppressed and harassed their lives. They cried out openly and emphatically in depression, despair and seemingly utter hopelessness. In the context of worship and belief, they came clean before God about their doubts, disappointments and deepest fears. At times their feelings of frustration and anger seem to border on vengeful rage. In my own dark night I counted more than fifty psalms written at times of deep personal trial and emotional turmoil. Read these and you find people wrestling before God. They expressed their feelings freely before the Lord while struggling to hold onto faith and hope in the midst of difficulty. Consider the following example:

> How long, O LORD? Will you forget me forever?
>   How long will you hide your face from me?
> How long must I wrestle with my thoughts
>   and every day have sorrow in my heart?
>   How long will my enemy triumph over me?
>
> Look on me and answer, O LORD my God.
>   Give light to my eyes, or I will sleep in death;
> my enemy will say, "I have overcome him,"
>   and my foes will rejoice when I fall.
>
> But I trust in your unfailing love;
>   my heart rejoices in your salvation.
> I will sing to the LORD,
>   for he has been good to me.
>
> Psalm 13

Abandonment, compulsive thoughts, depression and enemy attacks are taking a toll, and the psalmist, in essence, asks, "Where are You, God?" He confesses his deepest concerns while choosing to hold onto faith in hope of future deliverance.

I found it helpful at one point to express my fears by praying through Psalm 55. David revealed his own desire to run away from life to a place where no one would find him. Since I had felt like that myself, this psalm opened the door to an honest encounter with my own terror and the promised help of the living God. David wrote:

> Listen to my prayer, O God,
>   do not ignore my plea;
>   hear me and answer me.

> My thoughts trouble me and I am distraught
>> at the voice of the enemy,
>> at the stares of the wicked;
> for they bring down suffering upon me
>> and revile me in their anger.
>
> My heart is in anguish within me;
>> the terrors of death assail me.
> Fear and trembling have beset me;
>> horror has overwhelmed me.
> I said, "Oh, that I had the wings of a dove!
>> I would fly away and be at rest—
> I would flee far away
>> and stay in the desert;
> I would hurry to my place of shelter,
>> far from the tempest and storm."
>
> Psalm 55:1–8

I had struggled to hide these very feelings, ashamed and afraid they would disqualify me from ministry. But they were there just the same, tearing my insides apart. David taught me to open up before the Lord and express every fear and terror. He also taught me to move on, embrace the truth of God's love and cast every care upon Him (see verse 22).

What Do Our Emotions Tell Us?

Tremper Longman III and Dan Allender have written an important book about emotions called *The Cry of the Soul* (NavPress, 1994). In this work the authors discuss the critical link between emotions and spiritual well-being. They use the Psalms as the biblical foundation for their central thesis that emotions reveal how we are really doing with God. Feelings, according to Longman and Allender, signal our spiritual condition and tell us a great deal about what we really believe deep within.[1] Listening to our feelings and expressing them properly can be the doorway to spiritual growth. Why? Because emotions can point out the questions, misbeliefs and weak points in our faith.

The authors write:

> We can . . . view our emotions from the perspective of whether they lead us to engagement with God or move us away from greater dependence on Him. We can listen to what they tell us about our struggles. Emotions are like messengers from the front line of the battle zone. Our tendency is to kill the messenger. But if we listen carefully, we will learn how to fight the war successfully.
>
> Therefore, don't assume that resolving your turbulent emotions is the key to meeting God. It is actually within the inner mayhem of life that a stage is built for the intrusive story of His light and hope. God meets you in your weakness, not in your strength. He comforts those who mourn, not those who live above desperation. He reveals Himself more often in darkness than in the happy moments of life.[2]

Howard and Becky Taylor were going through a difficult time in their marriage. Several factors contributed to the upheaval, not least of which the fact that they were in deep financial need. Howard owned and operated a janitorial business that had provided for them comfortably for years. But recent economic trends had turned out disastrously for the business, and Howard was down to only fifteen hours of work per week. As a result they had to go on federal relief until things turned around for them.

One day Howard and Becky came over to our home for some prayer and support. They told Cheryl and me that the situation was putting a real strain on their marriage. Howard admitted he was still hurting from an angry verbal outburst that Becky sent his way only days before. Not only was the conflict fresh; it was still unresolved. We encouraged them to speak openly about the situation in hopes of bringing understanding and reconciliation.

Becky admitted to the angry barrage, saying she was worried about the bills. With four teenage children, their needs were real and constant. Becky had been thinking about every possible disaster and ended up launching on Howard. She told him it was all his fault and that he was not doing enough to resolve the situation. Howard was hurt and angry as a result.

But as we talked, Becky admitted it was not really Howard's fault. He was doing everything he could to change the situation, including continuing his education in order to seek new employment. Becky said she was just scared and frustrated. We expressed understanding and prayed for them both. Most importantly we asked Becky to think about what her feelings were signaling about her belief in God.

Becky admitted she had not even considered that issue. But right there she opened up to some serious heart-searching. "I guess I don't believe He is going to take care of us," she said. "I know that's wrong, but I think that's how I genuinely feel." This honesty brought Becky and Howard face to face with the true condition of their faith. They saw they needed to confess their doubts, asking God for both forgiveness and help. They saw a weakness in a foundational issue of belief and were able now to address it head on with the Holy Spirit's help.

Emotions are a window to the condition of your heart. You need to look carefully at the truths they expose. As you do, you will discover specific areas in which you need to align yourself with the will and ways of God. Admittedly, this is not easy and it takes time. It demands facing the pain and upheaval courageously in order to uncover the secrets your feelings hold. But in the end you will be free to move on to a deeper relationship with God, because you learned to be attentive to the alarm your emotions were sounding.

When We Fail to Respond Properly

Earlier I mentioned that failing to understand your emotions or express them properly can lead to serious problems. In fact, it can invite even greater emotional turmoil and potential spiritual bondage. I want to discuss several examples of this, which I hope will motivate you further to embrace a more biblical response to emotional turmoil. While God's way of handling your feelings leads to growth and freedom, your reaction can, in the long run, invite serious harm to your life.

Emotional Breakdown

I remember my father and grandfather standing in our backyard practicing archery. They were members of a sportsmen's club and participated regularly in tournaments. Their nightly ritual excited me as a small boy. I remember the beautiful bows, fine leather quivers and arrows with brightly colored feathers. I asked a thousand questions, especially, "Can I try? Can I shoot? Please?"

The day finally came for me to take my place in front of the target. I had received a small bow and arrow set and could hardly wait to let the arrows fly. But first came some very important instructions. Dad told me not to shoot at anything but the target and never to shoot an arrow straight into the air. (While I nodded yes, I violated his advice at both points rather quickly.) He also instructed me to refrain from pulling the bow and letting it go when there was no arrow on the string.

It was years before I understood this admonition or the important principle behind it. If a person "dry-fires" a wooden bow, they chance damaging its limbs. In fact, if it is done repeatedly, it is possible to shatter the bow. You see, pulling a bow string and letting it go creates tremendous energy. The arrow is meant to receive this energy, sending it flying toward the intended target. When that happens, the bow is safe and sound, sending all the force of the *twang* into the arrow. But shooting a bow without an arrow demands that the bow absorb all the energy within its limbs. A bow is not built for such shock, putting it at great risk. In some cases the energy simply breaks the bow because it had no arrow to receive the power.

Expressing emotions is like shooting an arrow. Energy is able to be expelled through the feelings of sorrow, anger, joy or laughter. But people who deny and stuff their emotions are keeping the energy pent up inside. Sooner or later breakdown will occur because the ongoing stress is too much for the system. You were made to emote, and when you do not, serious problems eventually result.

Many people experience emotional breakdown, as I did, precisely because they did not address and express their feelings properly. Initially they may think it was that one, most recent event that caused the breakdown. But the truth is, a lifetime of denial ultimately fractured their lives. Life is tough, and it does not help hiding your feelings. God wants them out in the light where you can use them properly as steppingstones to maturity and well-being.

Addiction

Most of us hate pain and will do almost anything to kill it. Unfortunately, what we choose to numb ourselves with is more perilous than facing the pain ever is. We trade short-term peace for long-term destruction. The choice of painkillers varies from person to person. My drug of choice was performance and workaholism. Others become addicted to activities like gambling, drinking, doing drugs, shopping, stealing or a host of other behaviors that anesthetize bad feelings. Instead of pressing through unpleasant pain to the source of conflict, people indulge in regular doses of addictive behaviors in hopes of a short-term high. Deeper pain and spiritual bondage result.

Jason Chapman is in vocational Christian ministry. A solid Bible expositor and teacher with a fine reputation as a senior pastor, he and I spent time together at a conference in the Midwest discussing current trends in church ministry. The conversation related for the most part to professional issues. As hard as I tried to move the dialogue to a personal level, Jason moved it back to the language of "religious business." Finally I decided to approach Jason head on.

"What's going on with you?" I asked. "Every time I get close to your heart, you run. Is something wrong?"

Jason looked flustered and told me he had been struggling for some time with lustful thoughts. He had been afraid to share this with anyone, fearing rejection or disqualification from ministry. But our friendship provided a safe enough context for Jason to risk at least limited honesty.

The conference setting provided the opportunity for numerous talks. Jason wanted some way to get free, and quickly. He asked about deliverance, Scriptures to memorize and tips on behavior modification. But my interest lay beneath the behavior at the level of his feelings. I suggested to Jason that he was using lust as a painkiller. It would be important for us to find the place of emotional turmoil and deal with the issues before the Lord.

It did not take long to link Jason's problem with lust to what had originally amplified the problem. Jason had begun struggling around the same time as serious opposition arose from a small group in his church. This revelation opened the door for us to discuss his true feelings about the conflict. He shared honestly and painfully about experiencing a sense of rejection, betrayal and failure. We took time praying about his hurt, asking God to heal the wound and help Jason stand firm in His love, faithfulness and eternal acceptance. This took time and was not pretty. But it was very healing and led to freedom and spiritual growth for Jason.

Addictive behavior can be a dark and destructive bondage. But freedom demands a deeper work that includes emotional integrity. You must express the feelings that bring pain in a context that is safe and in a way that leads to greater understanding of the underlying root issues.

Desolation

One of the saddest incidents in all of Scripture is found in 2 Samuel 13. It is the story of tragic events within the family of David. The account shows the devastating effects of failing to address and properly express powerful negative emotion. One of these outcomes was a life of perpetual depression and hopelessness for a young girl who was never given permission to grieve a personal crisis.

The story begins with Amnon, one of the sons of David, confessing to a friend that he was in love with his own sister Tamar. Amnon was frustrated that there was no apparent way to get close to her. But his shrewd friend, Jonadab, devised a plan that lured Tamar into Amnon's bedroom. She came at the instruction of her father, David, who had been deceived into thinking his son was ill. Tamar was sent there to care for her brother.

Once Tamar was in the bedroom, Amnon grabbed her and said, "Come to bed with me, my sister" (verse 11). The beautiful Tamar resisted, begging her brother not to do such a wicked thing. But he forced her into submission and raped her. Following the abuse, Amnon spoke words of hatred and rejection to his sister and had her forcibly removed from his presence.

Tamar was desperately hurt and violated. She ran away weeping loudly, and her brother Absalom saw her. When he asked Tamar what had happened, she told him everything. Then Absalom gave her advice that ruined her hopes of overcoming this tragedy. He said, "Be quiet now, my sister. . . . Don't take this thing to heart" (verse 20). In other words, "Stuff your feelings and pretend it never happened." The final word about Tamar, who obeyed her brother, is that she was "a desolate woman" (verse 20).

Countless people live in chronic despair and hopelessness because they failed to address and express the painful emotions that come with wounding. Fearing shame and rejection, they hide their feelings and the details of their abuse. But although silence appears to be a pathway to safety, it is an invitation to slow death. The pain eats away at an individual's emotional and spiritual well-being like a cancer. Despair, hopelessness and depression become constant companions that color the world a dull gray.

Wholeness and freedom are possible, on the other hand, by the power of the Holy Spirit. Jesus died for your wounds, whether physical, spiritual or emotional, and He provides the necessary power for healing. But what is hidden must be brought out into the light. Again, you need a safe environment in which to express your feelings, address the wounds and move on to embrace the promises of God's love and care.

Destruction

The story of Tamar and Amnon does not end with Tamar's desolation. Internalizing the events led to disaster that affected David's entire family.

King David had heard about the violation and "was furious" (verse 21), but he did nothing. Absalom, for his part, never said a word to Amnon. He, too, stuffed everything inside, which bred great hatred and animosity toward his brother. For two years Absalom remained silent about the rape, growing in his bitterness and plans for revenge. Finally the opportunity came to repay Amnon for the disgrace he had brought Tamar.

At sheepshearing Absalom prepared a great banquet and invited all his brothers. By this time everyone thought all had been forgotten, so Amnon came. When Amnon was nearly drunk with wine, Absalom gave the order for his brother's death. Absalom's friends rose up and killed Amnon, satisfying Absalom's deep hatred.

Not only did this cause deep heartache in the king's family, but Absalom had to flee to another land, where he lived for three years before considering reconciliation with his father. When Absalom did return, his father failed to discipline him properly for his sin. David simply acted as if it had never happened. This unhealthy avoidance and denial further compromised the relationship between them, allowing Absalom to redirect his deep anger toward his father. He soon rebelled against David and, in the end, was killed by one of the king's men. While silence may have offered short-term peace for David and his family, in the end it brought nothing but brokenness and death.

Absalom should have worked through his feelings immediately, but chose to be silent and stew alone. Eventually he reacted in destructive sin that only made the problem worse.

Many people do great harm to one another because they choose to react to pain rather than respond to it. Every day abuse occurs in homes where fathers and mothers fail to work through their feelings. Hurt and anger build until they are vented in destructive ways, and in the end things are much worse. Reacting to pain merely gives birth to more pain, whereas responding to pain opens the way to true healing and personal growth.

The journey through difficulty and trial engages your feelings powerfully. As much as it may hurt, emotional upheaval can be addressed properly and even open the way to spiritual growth and blessing. But it takes a commitment on your part to respond and not react to your feelings.

Move to express hurt, anger, fear, jealousy, despair and shame in ways that are consistent with the Word of God, following the example of your Lord Jesus and the psalmists. You dare not delay finding a safe context to share what lies deep inside. Work out your feelings before God in prayer in order to receive His comfort and strength. And finally, move beyond your own desires to embrace the will of God for the circumstances. These steps will lead to greater emotional health and continued growth in the Lord.

For Further Reading

The Cry of the Soul by Tremper Longman III and Dan Allender
Emotions, Can You Trust Them? by James Dobson
Why Am I Afraid to Tell You Who I Am? by John Powell
Healing for Damaged Emotions by David A. Seamands
Shame and Grace by Lewis Smedes
Heartfelt Change by Les Carter

7

Forgiveness Releases You from Torment

athy Tillman arrived at our home unexpectedly. We were surprised to see her, particularly since she and her husband, Matt, lived more than ten hours away by car. They had been close friends when we lived in Pennsylvania, but since we moved, our contacts had grown infrequent. Cheryl and I were glad to see Cathy, but the look on her face told us she was hurting badly.

We all shed plenty of tears that day as Cathy shared the details of her sudden entrance into a truly dark night. Matt, a gifted orthopedic surgeon, was being sued by one of his patients. The issue was ethical malpractice because of sexual immorality. Matt had become involved with this patient. When he finally acknowledged his sin and ended the affair, the woman responded with a lawsuit, stating that Matt had violated the patient/doctor relationship to his own advantage. Cathy had found out about it only the day before. What complicated matters even more was the fact that his license to practice medicine could be suspended, and the civil suit would be a matter of public record. Cathy was devastated and undone. She came to us for help and ended up staying more than a week.

Those days were not easy for any of us. Cathy was deeply hurt and very angry. I talked to Matt by telephone and he was scared to death. He wanted to join Cathy at our home, but she would not even consider it. She told us in no uncertain terms that the marriage was over and that she never wanted to see Matt again.

Initially all Cheryl and I did was listen and pray. We gave Cathy lots of space to vent her deep pain and anger. Compassion and understanding had to be the foundation of our ministry to her if we hoped to move her beyond the hurt to healing. Day after day we shared Scriptures about God's love and prayed that His presence would be real and constant in this time of weakness. As always, He was faithful to minister profoundly to Cathy.

After days of prayer and support, the time came to talk to Cathy about forgiveness. I knew it was not going to be easy. Cheryl and I moved cautiously, allowing Cathy time to deal with her feelings about this betrayal. Finally the moment came to talk with her about a plan for reconciliation that included biblical forgiveness.

Cathy responded in anger. "How could you even suggest forgiveness after what he did?" she demanded. She went on to list all the reasons Matt should pay for what he had done to her. Cathy was emotional, and I felt bad about stirring her up. But I knew forgiveness was not only God's will but critical to her emotional and spiritual well-being. It was the only way she could live free of this pain in the future.

So I told Cathy there were several key reasons to extend forgiveness to Matt. First, it is the way God has treated us in our own deep sin. Second, I reminded her that we are commanded in Scripture to forgive, no matter how many times a person offends us. Third, I talked at length about how unforgiveness imprisons a person in his or her own anger. Resentment and bitterness, I told Cathy, would choke the very life from her if she did not forgive Matt. In the end she would hurt more for her unforgiveness than from Matt's unfaithfulness.

It took some time before Cathy softened her heart to God's will, trusting that He would help her do the right thing. We guided Matt and Cathy toward reconciliation that included ongoing counseling and accountability. Today, years later, they are together and ministering in a local church in the East. While the medical board did revoke Matt's license to practice medicine for a probationary period, he was able to return to his profession with a renewed commitment both to Cathy and to the ethical requirements of his practice. More important, they passed through the dark night into a new day as husband and wife. Forgiveness was a big part of that victory.

Some Facts about Forgiveness

God's Word emphasizes the direct relationship between forgiveness and personal well-being.[1] The importance of forgiveness, Jesus taught, cannot be overstated or its practice overdone. It is God's way with penitent people and it needs to be our way, too. Forgiveness is the doorway to incredible peace. And, conversely, unforgiveness is a guaranteed formula for emotional and spiritual torment (see Matthew 18:34).

I want to challenge you, then, to consider several aspects of forgiveness as part of your own journey toward spiritual and emotional wholeness. Each dimension contributes a vital element to well-being and must be embraced prayerfully and acted upon practically along the way to freedom and maturity. The Holy Spirit will empower you to practice forgiveness in even the most difficult of situations. Six preliminary considerations are in order.

First, forgiving someone who has hurt you deeply often seems impossible. At times a powerful emotional resistance holds us back from even trying. You may have experienced this. One common hesitation stems from the misconception that forgiveness somehow erases the offender's responsibility. This is not true. Forgiveness removes the moral hindrance that stands between you and your abuser, leaving the consequences in God's hands. In addition, wounded people often see their bitterness or hatred as a shield to protect them from being hurt again. But for Christians, God is our Protector and the love of Christ our model.

A second preliminary consideration is that we may not realize unforgiveness actually damages *us*, the offended. Failure to forgive, Jesus said, places us in the hands of the tormentors (see Matthew 18:21–35). Unwillingness to forgive, no matter how horrible the offense, leads to personal torment—anger, bitterness, fear, revenge, jealousy or depression. Instead of keeping your victimizer the prisoner of your unforgiveness, you keep yourself. This is why it is important that you pour out your emotional pain before the Lord, and then, in the power of Christ, extend forgiveness freely. Forgiving sets *you* free.

Third, accept the fact that forgiveness involves a certain degree of risk, including the possibility of being hurt again. If you forgive an unfaithful spouse, there is the chance he or she could be unfaithful again. If the abuse you suffered recurs, you may need to remove yourself from the situation, while still extending forgiveness for the past offense.

Fourth, forgiving is not forgetting. Our brain functions to retain a record of past events. When the Holy Spirit touches our hearts, moving us to forgive, the pain of the past event often leaves, or at least it no longer drives us to unhealthy reactionary behavior. But the memory remains and is easily recalled, especially when we are placed in

131

similar circumstances. This can be a blessing in that it causes us to remember God's grace in a difficult moment of our past. But totally forgetting what happened is unlikely, and not a biblical condition of true forgiveness.

Fifth, forgiving is not excusing. It is not rationalizing away your abuser's responsibility because of the extenuating circumstances that led to your victimization. True, many perpetrators were themselves victims, and our hearts should reach out with hope for their healing. A sexual addiction, for example, may not be the person's fault. Sexual abuse or the absence of intimacy in childhood may have led him to the dysfunction. But his abusive actions are still his responsibility. Forgiveness means removing the hindrance, not rationalizing away the offense or the offender's responsibility.

Finally, forgiveness is not pretending that the event never happened. Some counselors and pastors use an unbiblical form of visualization in inner healing. They encourage people to return to the event in their minds, picturing Jesus undoing what happened. They call this "changing the pictures" on the walls of one's memory. This is both unbiblical and unhealthy. Jesus can heal the emotional scars caused by rape, but He does not rewrite history so that a woman can give a testimony of being unraped. Your history stands as it is. But Jesus can heal the wounds of victimization, giving you the power to say with sincerity, "I am free, and in the name of Jesus I set you free. You are forgiven."

The Healing Dimensions of Forgiveness

Any discussion of forgiveness must begin with your own sin against the holiness of God. Scripture is clear: Every one of us has broken the laws of God and falls short of righteousness (see Romans 3:23). Jeremiah wrote that the heart of man "is deceitful above all things and beyond cure" (Jeremiah 17:9). Before we are regenerated, we are wicked to the core of our beings, living in open rebellion before the Lord. Our best efforts apart from Christ are an abomination, full of selfishness and pride. And the consequence is one thing: eternal death (see Romans 6:23).

But God, full of love, sent Jesus Christ to die for our sin. He paid for our rebellion at the price of His own life. On the cross Christ canceled the debt held against us so we could be forgiven (see Colossians 2:13–15). He provided total redemption through His blood and the forgiveness of every sin (see Ephesians 1:7).

Consider this for a moment. We, the offenders, have been forgiven by the offended, not because of anything we did, but because of what He did. We are clean and pure as an act of His love and grace. We deserved death, but through Christ Jesus God gives us eternal life.

Jesus illustrates this truth beautifully through the parable of the Prodigal Son (see Luke 15:11–32). The son rebels against his father, leaves home and squanders his inheritance in wickedness. Then, broken and naked, he turns back toward home, hoping for a servant's portion of grace. His father, seeing him, runs with joy to meet him. The son begins to beg for mercy, but the father overpowers his plea with love and generosity. The youth is reinstated to full sonship, cleansed and clothed in a royal robe. The father declares it a day of celebration and the feast begins.

This parable is a window into the heart of God, our heavenly Father. At the slightest turning away from sin, He mercifully receives even the greatest sinner. Full forgiveness is found in Christ and complete sonship granted by grace. We are cleansed and crowned with honor instead of being punished and rejected. This is God's way, and it should never cease to humble and amaze us.

There are two immediate implications to this wonderful act of God's love. First, if He can forgive us, we should forgive ourselves. Many people struggle with failure and often punish themselves when they fail. If they make a mistake, an internal emotional mechanism kicks in, demanding payment. When the failure is mild, the punishment is less severe. Possibly they will berate themselves verbally or intentionally withhold some pleasure. When the failure is more severe, some people actually do physical harm to themselves. One of my counselees told of punching himself and beating his head against a wall. My wife has a friend who, when overrun with feelings of failure, slices her hands with razor blades. Her intention is not suicide, just enough pain to atone for her mistake.

Satan loves to motivate us to self-rejection and abuse. But the cross of Christ is our forever freedom from punishment. Jesus has borne the full wrath of God for our sin; no additional payment is necessary. When we fail, the Lord simply calls us to turn toward Him and move on to obedience. We must trust His grace that says, "It is finished." We are forgiven!

The second implication of this wonderful act of God's love is that His forgiveness should motivate us to be equally forgiving of others, regardless of the offense. Remember, no matter what someone has done to you, it cannot compare with your own sin against the holiness of almighty God. If He can forgive you, you can forgive those who have sinned against you. As we consider another's sin, let's be humble enough to recognize that we have the potential to commit the same offense. We are no less prone to sin and, given the same circumstance, are capable of anything—absolutely anything.

I must confess, there have been times when people offended me that I thought, *I could never do that to someone.* The Lord showed me that this is a self-deception rooted in self-righteousness. He reminded me that I am part of a sinful race, and whatever another has done, I, too, could do. Only His grace holds me back from the same hideous act. This thought gives birth to more compassion than condemnation, enabling me to move toward others on the common ground of God's grace. We who have been forgiven a great debt are called to forgive in response. It is the way of our Lord and the pathway to true peace.

Whenever you struggle with forgiveness, ask the Lord to show you the depth of your own sin that He has mercifully cleansed. Forgiving someone else pales in comparison.

Do Not Move to Forgiveness Too Quickly

As my sister and I were growing up, our parents made it crystal clear that jumping on beds was unacceptable. Mom left no question in our minds as to the consequence of breaking the household rules: The spankings would begin.

One day while Mom was in the basement doing wash, Bonny and I chose to chance it. We began to bounce with glee on our parents' bed—higher and higher, faster and faster, two children in joyful, reckless abandon! Suddenly Bonny, bouncing too close to the edge, came down with full force, hitting her tailbone on the corner of the footboard.

The pain must have been excruciating, for she cried out immediately, long and loud. I jumped to her side and began to beg, "Please don't cry, please! Laugh! Look at this funny face! Laugh! Ha, ha, ha!"

My goal was simple self-preservation. If she did not stop crying, Mom would hear, and that meant only one thing: Soon we would both be crying. I did everything

I could to silence Bonny's cries, in an effort to keep my own sin in hiding.

It did not work.

I have been in vocational Christian ministry for more than twenty years now. In all these years, from each of the different perspectives of ministry, one truth stands out: God's people are uncomfortable with vulnerability. When someone begins to express deep feelings of emotional turmoil, we often send the same message I did to my sister: "Please don't hurt. Not here, not now." Why? Because in some way it may bring to the surface our own hidden pain.

The people of Christ are made up of former liars, adulterers, fornicators, cheats, slanderers, bigots and addicts of all sorts. Before Christ, we all possessed the characteristics of the ungodly: anger, hatred, jealousy, envy, rage, malice. Every single member of the Body of Christ was at one point dead in sin. But through repentance and faith in Jesus Christ, our lives were transformed.

Once converted, every new believer is taught about holiness and godly living. Some learn these truths from an unbiblical base of legalism. Others are schooled in the glory of God's grace and unmerited favor that positionally give Christians righteousness, which transforms them day by day through the ongoing work of the Holy Spirit. Either way the message of the Church is clear. Sin in all forms is unacceptable and destructive.

But in far too many congregations, people respond to the call to holiness in a sinful and unhealthy manner: They hide and put on the cosmetic of religiosity. Although their private lives are inconsistent with the Christian faith, their public lives appear wonderfully in line with biblical maturity. They know the proper words, serve the church in the proper ways, sing the appropriate songs and attend the scheduled services faithfully. All the while they struggle with sin and past wounds, which eventually eat away at the core of their lives. Emotionally these believers are held together with chewing gum and bailing wire. Any disruption is capable of putting their entire pretense at risk.

The blame for this lies, in part, at the feet of church leadership. Shaming messages are too often communicated with this kind of rebuke: "Don't be caught in sin; it will cost you reputation, position in the local church and the admiration of fellow believers." Such pressure keeps people from openness and vulnerability. Behind the facade of perfection is a virtual thorn thicket of sin and pain. Believers are often afraid to open up for fear of rejection.

Darren came to our congregation with deep emotional wounding from an abusive childhood. For years he carried the memories of beatings from his father, open shaming, even being tied in a closet for hours as a form of punishment. Darren did not trust men, was confused about his identity and lived in constant fear. We led Darren into one of our growth groups, thinking it would be a place of acceptance and healing. Although scared to death, he took the risk.

Our growth groups begin by asking the Wesleyan question, "How are things with your soul?" When it came time for Darren, he opened up, sharing just the surface of his broken past. But group members became extremely uncomfortable with the high level of emotion. So, instead of listening and weeping with Darren over his deep pain, they tried to stuff what was happening. How did they do that? By insisting that he forgive.

You may say, "Well, isn't that the answer?" In due time, yes. But Darren was in deep pain and needed to be honest about his hurt and anger at his father, which were ruining his life. The people in the group, however,

137

instead of allowing him to mourn his loss, insisted that he move immediately to forgiveness.

In some cases true forgiveness comes only after an individual has released his or her pain before the Lord. Fellow believers should be patient, allowing the Holy Spirit to do that deeply needed work. But most Christians are too insecure to allow such vulnerability and honesty in their midst. Encouraging an atmosphere of emotional openness may cause other Christians to break through unexpectedly to their own pain. That fear motivates us to stuff our emotions, discouraging vulnerability in others. "Let's all just forgive and forget!"

The Church is not a haven for sinless saints. Though we are redeemed by Christ, there is a lot of deep work to be done in countless lives. But it requires openness and a safe atmosphere in which we can get in touch with our pain. When that happens, true forgiveness flows out like the river Christ intended. But encouraging a person to forgive before he or she has had the opportunity to pour out emotional pain at the cross of Christ is premature and unhealthy.

Learning to Forgive God

Let me begin by stating the obvious: God cannot and does not sin. His very nature is marked by perfect holiness in every attribute and action. God is perfect in love, mercy and grace. He is righteous, just and faithful. It is theologically impossible for anyone ever to point to God and call Him on any transgression. God is infinite in knowledge, wisdom and power, eternally good in all that He is and does. He cannot and does not sin. Let me repeat that: *God cannot and does not sin.*

But countless men, women and children in this world are angry at God. They feel let down by Him, abandoned or left unprotected at the times they needed Him most. Some people suppress their feelings while others are vocal, turning their backs on God in response to what they believe was failure on His part.

Let's face it: There is undeniable tension in the Christian life. Countless passages in Scripture assure believers of God's love, concern and protection. Christians are promised angelic care, divine intervention, shelter in times of storm and a yoke that is easy and light. Christian biographies are filled with wonderful tales of divine intervention in the hour of trial. The promises of God are true and should be embraced confidently by all believers. But many Christians face experiences that seem to contradict these truths. Through no fault of their own, Christian women are raped, Christian husbands die prematurely, Christian children suffer from terminal cancer, Christian senior citizens agonize with Alzheimer's disease and Christian families encounter all forms of violence.

Well-meaning pastors try to help by invoking Scriptures that assure God's sovereignty and the promise of ultimate good resulting from any and all tragedy. While some Christians are strong enough to hold to these truths, more nod their heads while suppressing deep-seated emotional rage: *Where were You, God? How could You let this happen to me?*

Most Christian victims sense that their feelings are inappropriate, so they stifle them, hoping that over time the pain will go away. This approach is encouraged, more often than not, by fellow believers: "Have faith, trust, believe, and everything will turn out just fine. Praise the Lord!"

But stifling emotions and failing to address the pain of victimization is unhealthy and unbiblical. Unhealthy in that suppressed anger shows its ugly head sooner or later in some other form. It may be depression or misdirected rage or fear. It may be performance, busyness or one of any number of addictions. Anger unaddressed and suppressed always leads to trouble. Pious platitudes, however correct theologically, are not the first steps to overcoming emotional wounding.

And suppressing anger, even when it is directed at God, is unbiblical. Take Job. For three-quarters of the book, he points his finger at God—not in a disrespectful or cursing way. But Job let God know that he considered his lot unjustified and unfair. In chapter 9 Job admits that no mortal can question God's actions because He is so great and mighty. But Job says, "If only there were someone to . . . remove God's rod from me, so that his terror would frighten me no more. Then I would speak up" (Job 9:33–35). Then Job says, "I will give free rein to my complaint" (Job 10:1), and he goes on to present his case. While recognizing God's wisdom, justice and righteousness, Job still cries out to God, "I've been wronged."

It is easy to find similar laments throughout the Psalms. In Psalm 77 the writer cries out with agony,

> "Will the Lord reject forever?
>   Will he never show his favor again?
> Has his unfailing love vanished forever?
>   Has his promise failed for all time?
> Has God forgotten to be merciful?
>   Has he in anger withheld his compassion?"
>
> verses 7–9

The Israelite was speaking from the depth of his wounded soul: "God, where are You?" He was emotionally wrought and, instead of suppressing his anger and pain, he let his complaint be known to God.

Christian victims who harbor suppressed anger against God must be encouraged to go before Him and say what they feel. While maintaining respect and honor, victims need to express what is going on inside, even if their feelings are based on a lie. They need to get it out and tell God what they may have been suppressing for years.

As a parent, I must make decisions at times that frustrate and even anger my children. I am secure enough and love them sufficiently to encourage them to vent. As long as they show respect, I want them to express their case, even with high emotion. After they are done, I attempt to show them my perspective, even while honoring their pain and helping them lovingly to work through to understanding.

God is the perfect Parent. Infinite in love and patience, He can take an emotional torrent aimed at Him from a finite, limited, yet greatly loved person. As that person expresses emotion, He honors him or her, moving in compassion and care. Then, through Scripture and the witness of the Holy Spirit, He reminds that person of His perfect perspective. Like Job, victims are schooled in His sovereignty and justice, and encouraged, like the writer of Psalm 77, to meditate on His past deeds. This emotional cleansing allows room for peace and inner healing.

Pretending damages emotional well-being. You must allow what is hidden to be made known. In the light, destructive lies are disarmed, and the tender touch of God brings transformation built on trust and truth. If you are angry at God, take your case before Him. It will open the way to a transforming encounter with the God of infinite love.

"As We Forgive Our Debtors"

While working through my own dark night, I asked the Holy Spirit to bring to my memory any and all events that were causing emotional and spiritual upheaval in my life. The Holy Spirit answered that prayer and gently began to bring to my mind memories of past woundings. It was a painful time. I did not realize just how much I had stuffed. Like many people, I had thrown a blanket of forgiveness over my past—in part because I had been instructed that this was the correct thing to do, and in part because I did not want to deal with the past.

Now, as the Holy Spirit put His finger on unresolved issues, I wrote them down on a tablet. Within several days the list became quite long, covering my life up to that point. It was easy to identify two categories of unresolved issues.

The first category was woundings that had occurred to me. Most, though not all, were from my childhood and adolescence. Some were more painful to recall than others—either direct assaults with intention to hurt or else unintentional abuses from people who did not really know better. The second category was hurts I had inflicted on others. (This is the focus of the next section.)

Over a period of time, the Lord led me to bring before Him each event. The process usually began as I remembered in some detail what had happened. As this unfolded in God's presence, pent-up emotions invariably began to flow. At times I experienced weeping, at other times anger over the violation. Because of the high emotion connected with these memories, I knew the issues were real and the wounds still there.

Regardless of the length of time it took to unleash these emotions before God, I sensed on the other end a singular necessary requirement. Time after time, event by event, regardless of the severity or intent of the wounding, the Lord called me to extend forgiveness. This is the way of the Father, taught and modeled by the Son and empowered by the Holy Spirit. At times I struggled with it, wanting a person to feel pain or remain a prisoner behind the bars of my own bitterness. But as soon as I stopped wrestling and rested the matter in God's hands, reaching out in genuine forgiveness, healing flowed in. The Holy Spirit's touch was always gentle, and freedom the result. Sometimes as I extended forgiveness, I actually felt the release of oppression inside.

Did I go to every person who had hurt me, bring up the issue and offer forgiveness? My answer may sound simplistic, but it is the way this process unfolded in my life. Whatever the Holy Spirit instructed—through His Word, through an inner witness or through a trusted counselor—that is what I did.

Generally I did not go to those who had wounded me unintentionally. The Lord enabled me to see through His eyes and release them. The memory remained, but now there was no pain, only compassion and understanding that could have come only from above.

Reconciliation for other woundings included godly confrontation. While I was growing up, for example, my dad was physically present but emotionally very distant. This took a toll on me and resulted in deep pain. In God's moment, as I was led sovereignly by the Spirit, a face-to-face, issue-by-issue meeting with my dad occurred. Because I had already dealt with the problem before the Lord, much of the pain and anger was already released. The talk was still risky and tough for both of us, but God had been at work in Dad's heart, too. As I talked, I could see that this powerful man, hardened by forty years in the coal mines, was both soft and sorrowful. I will *never* forget that time of reconciliation. It was holy, and we were both deeply touched. I love my dad and know he is a beautiful human being. I am proud to be his son!

Go and Reconcile with Your Brother

Our Lord is clear about a believer's responsibility when he or she offends another. We are to go to the person we offended, seek forgiveness and reconciliation and offer restitution. We looked in chapter 5 at Jesus' words in the Sermon on the Mount:

"If you are offering your gift at the altar and there remember that your brother has something against you, leave your gift there in front of the altar. First go and be reconciled to your brother; then come and offer your gift."

Matthew 5:23–24

The parable of the Prodigal Son illustrates the requirement of repentance and confession of sin, as well as the beauty of reconciliation. Further on in Luke we find the wonderful story of Zacchaeus. Transformed by the love of Christ, he seeks reconciliation and makes restitution with all offended parties. Seeking the forgiveness of God and others is unmistakably a requirement of a Kingdom lifestyle. It is also part of the journey toward emotional and spiritual wholeness.

As I mentioned earlier, the Holy Spirit did more than bring to my mind woundings at the hands of others. There was also a long list of offenses on my part. Partly rooted in dysfunction, partly in sinful habits, I had done many things to injure people. At first, as the Spirit brought these events to mind, I was puzzled. I had confessed my sins at the time of my conversion, and had since turned to the Advocate innumerable times for forgiveness. Were not these experiences forgiven, as the Scripture said, forgotten and cast "as far as the east is from the west" (Psalm 103:12)? What was it about these particular sins that seemed linked to my emotional turmoil? How were these memories connected with my journey through the valley of sorrow?

As I went before the Lord with these questions, He showed me a common element in each memory. The issues involved individuals I had in some way sinned against. While I may have sought the Father's forgiveness through Christ Jesus, I had never gone to the people themselves to confess and be reconciled. Through the Holy Spirit's conviction, I knew that the path toward my emotional wholeness must go by way of these people. Truthfully, it was probably the most frightening part of the journey, undoubtedly because of pride. But in the strength of the Lord I stepped forth.

Most of the issues involved those closest to me—sins against my parents, sister, wife, children and friends. Others were linked to co-workers and people from my past. In some cases the people involved knew and remembered the offenses. In other cases they did not know what I had done, making the situation tense at times.

One issue involved not people I knew, but a company. While connecting our antenna to the back of the television, I had noticed a cable. Attaching it, I found that it increased our reception from three to eight stations. I thought little about it at the time and just enjoyed the additional access. Now the Holy Spirit convicted me deeply that this was in fact stealing. Quickly I disconnected the cable. But the Lord wanted more. With my wife I traveled to the company office, confessed my sin to the staff and asked forgiveness. Then I paid double for the time period under question.

I mention this with embarrassment, yet thankful for the tough lesson. Sin hurts both the offender and the offended.

In the Lord's Prayer we are taught to extend forgiveness and to seek the same of others (see Matthew 6:12). Many moving through the dark night of depression, fear, bitterness, anger or countless other problems are suffering because of an inadequate understanding and practice of this Kingdom standard. If you are seeking emotional and spiritual wholeness, you must pass by this way. Forgiveness is an indispensible prerequisite to your genuine and lasting freedom.

For Further Reading

The Blood of the Cross by Andrew Murray
Written in Blood by Robert Coleman
The Search for Peace by Robert S. McGee and Donald W. Sapaugh
Forgive and Forget by Lewis Smedes
What's So Amazing about Grace? by Philip Yancey

Healthy Relationships Move You toward Spiritual Maturity

t would take a book even to begin to tell about the impact God's dear people have had on me in recent years. The story would start with my wife, who stayed her post when the bottom dropped out from under me. I would tell of my son and daughters, who daily extended grace and understanding in the face of my incredible weakness. I would share details of my parents' support as they came from Pennsylvania and stayed at our side for five dark months. Then there is my doctor, Tom, who called me every day for months with Scriptures of hope and healing. Tom, Patty, Sarah, Andy, Bonny—the names and stories would go on and on. Prayer, counsel, encouragement and practical help were but a small part of all they brought in the name of Jesus Christ to the moment. I will be forever grateful, and am more deeply convinced than ever that relationships are an indispensable part of Christian living.

There is no way I could have progressed along the precarious path to emotional and spiritual well-being apart from the help of my friends and family. Frankly, I would have lost my way without them. Every victory I now have is a direct result of their incredible commitment to stay right there with me through all the pain, heartache, purging and rebuilding. Over and again they served as the arms and legs of Christ, sometimes carrying and always encouraging me along the way to freedom and wholeness.

This pilgrimage called life is no private matter. It is a journey in community, and the wise invest much to have friends and family accompany them along the way.

Many of us want to get away from people when emotional and spiritual upheaval settles in. Some internal defense mechanism seems to engage, pushing the hurting and wounded into seclusion. Certain aspects of this are good, in that solitude can give space for proper healing. But there is a right and wrong way to respond to this desire.

The worst thing you can do is move into isolation, whether spiritual, emotional or physical. Isolation is a form of hiding motivated by the desire to avoid pain and escape any possibility of shame. It also allows problems to gain a greater foothold. Cut off from caring people, you must battle alone. The lies of the evil one are often constant and powerful. Without the counsel and support of other Christians, you become susceptible to great deception and potential destruction. Total withdrawal is never the right response to difficulty and trial.

The proper response is a selective hiddenness. This includes a healthy balance between biblical solitude and ongoing support from close friends and family. By solitude I mean extended periods of stillness that give space for God to speak. It involves retreating from people intentionally in order to be alone with God, to receive what only He can give you: words of love, direction and healing.

I want to emphasize your need for a supportive Christian community during the time of hiddenness brought on by seasons of pain and sorrow. While it is important to set clear boundaries with people so you are not relationally overrun, you must allow certain friends and family members ongoing access to your life. Their love, support, counsel and care are essential ingredients to your well-being, both emotional and spiritual. No matter how dark the night or long the journey, their presence is necessary if you are properly to traverse the ups and downs that come with trial. Such close people are there to cry with you, pray, speak truth and help you hold onto faith, especially when you are too tired, weak or confused to hold on alone. Most important, the supportive community is there to love you consistently and unconditionally, as Jesus would, reminding you of His ongoing forgiveness and hope. They are there to protect you from yourself and sometimes from the evil one.

Your supportive community should consist of Christian brothers and sisters who gather around you for mutual care and encouragement. They are not the crowd—that group of strangers you meet daily but do not know beyond formality. They are not the committee—that working group held together by formal structures of organization. No, the necessary people I am describing are the community of believers that comprises your closest companions, intimate friends growing to know one another on their way to knowing God. You need them and they need you. In supporting you along the difficult way of life, they, too, grow in spiritual stature and health. It is an unavoidable consequence of the interrelationship that belongs to true Christian community. In healthy relationships you and they change.

Scripture constantly reinforces the essential nature of community. Even the most casual reading of God's Word makes it clear that interdependence, not independence, is the way to wholeness. The book of Eccle-

siastes, for example, warns against friendlessness, rein-
forcing the importance of strong relationships:

> There was a man all alone;
>> he had neither son nor brother.
> There was no end to his toil,
>> yet his eyes were not content with his wealth.
> "For whom am I toiling," he asked,
>> "and why am I depriving myself of enjoyment?"
> This too is meaningless—
>> a miserable business!
>
> Two are better than one,
>> because they have a good return for their work:
> If one falls down,
>> his friend can help him up.
> But pity the man who falls
>> and has no one to help him up!
> Also, if two lie down together, they will keep warm.
>> But how can one keep warm alone?
> Though one may be overpowered,
>> two can defend themselves.
> A cord of three strands is not quickly broken.
>
> Ecclesiastes 4:8–12

This passage leaves little question about the importance of supporting relationships. Without them a person is sure to experience an empty, lonely life, while the
individual with friends finds fulfillment, support,
warmth and strength as his or her "good return." Unfortunately, countless Christians, although they do not realize it, are pursuing tragic loneliness because they are
not investing in true, biblical community.

The apostle Paul wrote repeatedly about the importance of relationship. Comparing Christians to a body,
he taught that each person is joined together, support-

ing one another and growing in the context of love (see Ephesians 4:16). He also said that in both suffering and joy, believers are so interrelated that what one experiences, the other does, too (see 1 Corinthians 12:26). The Body of Christ is to manifest neither isolation nor independence. Rather, God's people are to be forever united under the glorious headship of Jesus Christ.

Our Lord modeled interdependence during His life and ministry on earth. He surrounded Himself with a select group of men and women into whom He poured His life. They traveled together, ate, slept and trained as a group. What one experienced, all experienced. Jesus showed them the way of mutual support and service, calling them to *agape* love as the standard of commitment and behavior (see John 13:34). He sent them by twos into the world and promised always to be present in the context of corporate life.

In the first century, when an individual made a commitment to Christ, he or she also committed to the community of Christ. In our Western, highly individualistic mindset, we often miss the essential interrelationship between these two commitments. As a result, many of us try to follow the Lord apart from Christian community. In difficult times, such a choice is a guaranteed formula for disaster.

Presently I have very important relationships in my life, in the context of Spring Meadow, a retreat center my wife and I began for hurting people. Several wonderful people provide incredible support, encouragement and accountability to our ministry, as well as to Cheryl and me personally. I cannot imagine what life would be like without them! We have adopted Zephaniah 3:9 as our common commitment to Christian service: "Then will I purify the lips of the peoples, that all of them may call on the name of the LORD and serve him shoulder to shoulder."

Shoulder to shoulder is the only way to experience and reveal Christ to the world and stand firm against the evil one. Alone we perish, while united we do better than stand; we move on toward spiritual maturity and freedom.

All aspects of Christian community are important, but I want to discuss two issues in this chapter that are most relevant to the journey through the dark night: the necessity of finding a spiritual director and the dynamics of a healthy spiritual community.

Find a Wise Spiritual Director

Please do not let the term *spiritual director* intimidate you. Granted, it is not used much these days, but it is an age-old concept gaining renewed popularity in our day. The phrase refers to a mature Christian who offers advice and encouragement as part of a person's spiritual development. He or she serves as a spiritual father or mother, committed to guiding certain people toward greater intimacy with God and increased spiritual maturity.

Relational in nature, spiritual direction demands a high degree of shared life to be most effective. A spiritual director walks alongside you, helping you move toward Christlikeness. He or she points you toward the narrow way to God. You are a wise Christian if you recognize your need and submit humbly to this kind of spiritual counsel.

The History of Spiritual Direction

The concept of spiritual direction is, as I have said, not new. Throughout the centuries this ministry has enjoyed a wide variety of expressions. Time and space do not allow a thorough historical review, but a few comments may help put this discussion in context.

Biblically we learn of spiritual direction from the example of the Lord Jesus Himself. His ministry to the disciples involved the prayerful selection of His primary followers, time spent together in community, teaching and demonstrating principles of the Kingdom, empowering the disciples for effective service, ongoing supervision and sacrificial service. Jesus gave His life to His followers so that they would better find and follow God. They in turn went on to direct other believers by a similar model of ministry.

The apostle Paul served as spiritual director to Timothy. In his second letter to his young disciple, Paul refers to Timothy as his son. Theirs is obviously a spiritual relationship, with Paul the older, wiser and far more experienced believer. Timothy is zealous for the Lord but needs loving counsel to move ahead toward spiritual maturity. Paul's love and concern for Timothy come through in his letters, in which he guides Timothy tenderly yet emphatically toward following Jesus Christ. Paul encourages Timothy through tough times while affirming God's call and direction in his young life.

Every believer needs a Paul. And when the time is right, each Christian should find a Timothy to serve in return.

Some of the clearest examples of spiritual direction occurred in the fourth and fifth centuries—a period known as the time of the Desert Fathers. These men and women lived in the deserts of Egypt and Syria, detaching from society in order to attach more profoundly to God. Younger men submitted themselves to older, more mature "fathers," forming an often lifelong relationship. The spiritual father spent time with the disciple, pointing him to God and shaping the inner attitudes and behaviors that were most consistent with holiness and purity. These early Christians believed that life's journey was hazardous at best and should never be made without a guide. Spiritual fathers were to lead by example in an attitude of humility and love.

This expression of spiritual direction seems extreme for our society, but we can learn from it. The Desert Fathers teach us that the impact of the world, the flesh and the devil is profound and powerful. Standing fast and faithful demands radical separation unto God and a commitment to learn from mature men and women who have moved toward Christ ahead of us. The Desert Fathers teach us that true Kingdom life is caught more than it is taught. They show us that submitting to one another must go beyond words to experienced reality.

I am drawn personally to the writings of the Christian mystics of the twelfth to eighteenth centuries. While one must read with discernment, the literature of these saints has much to offer us. Many of the published works were actually letters or essays of spiritual direction sent to the disciples of their time. People like Theresa of Avila, Saint Bonaventure, Saint Francis, Fénelon, Madame Guyon and Jean-Pierre de Caussade offer rich guidance for the Christian life. Most important, they reinforce the importance of shared life as a vehicle of spiritual vitality. These men and women not only submitted to direction, but committed themselves to helping others discover the voice of God in the events of daily life.

Patterns of Spiritual Direction

As I have stated, there have been many different patterns of spiritual direction throughout history. Sometimes an informal relationship developed between two people, based on mutual respect and love, in which a younger person volunteered to submit his life to the direction of a spiritual father. There were also formal structures of formation, in which an older, more mature believer was assigned a new disciple by a local body of believers. I experienced this as a young pastor. The denomination assigned me to an experienced pastor, who helped me lovingly to navigate the often stormy seas of ministry, pointing out God amid the pitfalls of pastoral life. There has also been a more institutional approach to spiritual direction represented by the monastic life—communities dedicated to spiritual disciplines and direction as the best pathway to experience God.

For most of us, the best approach is an informal one. Prayerfully seek out a spiritual father or mother and submit willingly and regularly to his or her humble guidance. (I will say more in a moment about the role and qualifications of an effective spiritual director.) At times a more formal approach is helpful, especially when the seasons and issues of life are particularly complex.

My role at Spring Meadow is that of spiritual director. People come for a stated period of time seeking rest, renewal and restoration. I meet with them to help discern God in the midst of their present trials. The relationship is limited by time and context, providing a sort of intensive care direction during seasons of crisis and pain.

What Is the Role of the Spiritual Director?

The spiritual director, simply described, helps you grow in intimacy with God and in personal holiness. While there are many ways in which this development takes shape, three are most important. First, the spiritual director helps you find God in the midst of day-to-day trials and struggles. God is involved intimately and actively in your life, coming to you in the circumstances and trials set before you. The spiritual director encourages you to ask, "Where are You, God, in all of this, and what are You saying to me?"

Second, the spiritual director helps you recognize the voice of God. The noise of society often drowns out the whispers of the Lord. The spiritual director teaches you to grow still and wait for His revealed word. As such, he or she often leads you into the vital disciplines of solitude, prayer and spiritual reading. By example the director guides you into seasons of rest, quiet and waiting, teaching you and me how to say, "Speak, Lord, Your servant is listening."

Finally, the spiritual director encourages you to respond to the voice of God that comes through trial. My initial reaction to trial was to run as fast as I could to escape the cloud of unknowing. The seasoned spiritual director encourages you to stand in the storm, waiting for revelation and clear instructions. Once you perceive God's purposes, the spiritual director will help you surrender in loving obedience to the Father's will. In my case, I heard God call me away from "importance" and into intimacy. The role of the spiritual director was to encourage me to say yes, regardless of the cost, and then to meet God at the point of obedience and surrender.

There are many casualties in the Christian life, precisely because believers are too proud to ask for help and too afraid to submit their lives to someone. As a result, many traveling the path of pain and suffering miss the treasures that lie buried along the way—treasures meant to empower their lives and set them free to know God more intimately and serve Him more joyfully. A qualified spiritual director will help you mine the hidden riches, not miss them.

Qualifications of a Spiritual Director

It should be obvious by now that not just anyone can serve you as spiritual director. It takes a person of recognized maturity who possesses essential qualities of

Christian spirituality. In general, these men and women must be experienced in the Christian life, having navigated the terrain of trial with humble effectiveness. They should be discerning, disciplined in matters of spirituality and clearly walking in the Spirit. They should be good examples, with patient dispositions and keen sensitivity to people's needs and God's provision.

I see three essential qualities of effective spiritual directors. They must be open and vulnerable about their own Christian pilgrimages. This includes sharing the lessons of defeat as well as of victory. Second, they must be men and women of prayer—not just regular intercession but ongoing communion and contemplation before the Lord. Finally, qualified spiritual directors are people of love. They must lead by humble example, not lording people into submission by command, but by the force of irresistible love.

Are such people out there? Yes, but the very nature of their lives sets them apart from public acknowledgment. They live quiet yet powerful lives, and are best discovered by asking God to lead you to them or them to you. They are probably not the charismatic superstars who gather crowds. Rather, they are the servant-leaders who always put others out in front of themselves. They are not necessarily in professional ministry and probably do not refer to themselves by the term we are using here. Yet these people have hearts for God and a humble willingness to invest their lives in others.

Prayerfully find one and then ask if he or she would walk with you down the path of life, pointing out God's presence in the landscape of your own personal journey. Be patient in the relationship; it takes time to develop the necessary trust and respect. But over time, doors will begin to open and riches of wisdom will pass between the two of you.

Find a Healthy Spiritual Community

It is not hard to find gatherings of Christians in our society. But a group of believers does not necessarily make a spiritual community. There are many local churches, small groups and working committees that are exclusively Christian; yet in far too many cases the driving force is a religious agenda, and the relationship level is shallow, characterized by a hiddenness that borders on hypocrisy. These groups are spiritually powerless and likely to do more harm than good.

If you desire support, encouragement, counsel and accountability, become part of a truly spiritual community.[1] By *spiritual* I mean a place where God is welcomed and His Spirit is free to move, actively changing people into the likeness of Jesus Christ. By *community* I mean a gathering of people biblically interdependent and committed to one another as they journey through life. This may be a local church or small group. It may be your family, friends or weekly prayer group. Whatever it is, a spiritual community is a place where the Lord is at work in people's lives, and people are truly there for one another along the way.

Every believer needs to be part of a healthy spiritual community. It is not always easy. A spiritual community is still made up of people, and we get under one another's skin. Our individual problems and personalities make for interesting and at times exasperating situations. With the Holy Spirit's help, however, these stumblingblocks to harmony actually become steppingstones to change. Our "stuff" gets right out in the open where we can all work on it.

What makes this possible are the necessary ingredients of shared life that I now want to discuss. What follows represents the goal toward which the spiritual community commits itself, knowing that the practical expression of each ingredient takes time and patience to develop properly.

A Christ-Centered Community

The truly healthy spiritual community is thoroughly Christ-centered. Jesus' life, death and resurrection are at the very core of the words and witness of each member. Jesus is recognized, worshiped and obeyed as Lord and Savior. Knowing Him and growing to be like Him are the very reasons for existence; and, following the admonition of Scripture, all eyes and hearts are focused on Him.

In John 17:3 Jesus said that knowing Him is the way to know the Father, and knowing them both is the key to eternal life. In the healthy spiritual community, intimacy with Christ is a prioritized part of the corporate experience, whether through learning from the gospels, remembering Jesus' sacrifice, retelling His work in each other's lives or experiencing His presence in prayer. Jesus Christ is the ruling principle and passion of shared life. All attitudes, appetites and actions, personal or corporate, are evaluated in light of His wonderful life and Kingdom precepts.

Put simply, in the healthy spiritual community Jesus Christ is clearly and identifiably the living Lord.

A Spirit-Filled Community

The help and change we all need does not come by mere human effort. It demands a supernatural transaction accomplished by the presence and power of the Holy Spirit. He is God-with-us, involved in everything it means to be a Christian. The Spirit is active at conversion, infilling our lives. He is the agent of sanctification, the distributor of spiritual gifts and the power present for victorious Christian living. There is no experience of God apart from Him and no transformation without His touch.

The healthy spiritual community submits to the Holy Spirit and actively welcomes His presence. Dependence on Him is the shared commitment of every member. The Holy Spirit is the recognized Teacher, Counselor, Guide, Comforter and Friend. The healthy spiritual community prays for His outpouring and makes room for His coming through surrender, confession, unity and openness. The Spirit-filled and Spirit-directed life is seen as the privileged responsibility of all believers, both corporately and individually.

A Grace-Empowered Community

Legalism kills—it is that simple! Any notion that the blessings of the Christian life are earned by personal effort is both unbiblical and destructive. If a Christian group rewards people with love and acceptance when they act right and rejects them when they do wrong, that group does not have a clue about the true Gospel of Christ.

A healthy spiritual community understands and practices grace. Grace-based living means people believe that every good thing we are, have and hope to receive comes as a gift from God through faith in Christ. His blessings cannot be earned, they are not given conditionally and they have nothing to do with personal worthiness. Everything is a gift of love, provided unconditionally by a merciful and gracious heavenly Father. He turns rejects into righteous ones and sinners into saints.

People in a spiritual community are not accepted or rejected because of their behavior or status. Each and every member is recognized as an heir of God in Christ and encouraged to live a life consistent with the noble heritage God bestows on each person. In such a community we find encouragement instead of condemnation, and a clear call to serve Christ in response to His love rather than from the motivation of guilt. It is grace that sets the Christian free and grace that keeps him free.

A Vulnerable Community

If people are to grow, they need a safe place in which they can share the deep pain and struggles that weigh them down. It must be a place free from self-righteous judgment and pious platitudes. There must be openness, confidentiality, compassion, forgiveness and acceptance. It is a place where people are patient, understanding and honest. It needs to be a vulnerable gathering of fellow pilgrims.

A healthy spiritual community provides an atmosphere that encourages people to bring their issues out into the light of Christ's healing love. Every member recognizes the danger of pretense and the potential transformation of a genuine truth encounter. The goal is always freedom, and the power of strength through weakness the vehicle of Christ's healing touch.

An Available Community

A healthy spiritual community is there for its members, particularly in times of pain, trial and difficulty. Members are there to weep with the friend who weeps, to suffer as he or she suffers and to mourn when sorrow presses in. Availability might mean as little as listening over the telephone or as much as carrying the person who can go no farther on his or her own. Whatever is appropriate and genuinely needed, the community seeks to provide in the strength and name of Jesus Christ.

The goal of such support is not rescuing people from the dark night. Rather, members seek to support each other through the storms and floods and fires of life.

161

They commit to helping each member find God in the moment of trial, and stand with them until the light of His presence is known. An available community makes people feel more secure along the precarious path toward spiritual well-being.

A Praying Community

We all know that life is not easy. The uncertainties we face on our own can create uncontrollable anxiety and worry. The trials and difficulties of day-to-day living can bring even the strongest men or women to their knees. But once there, they are finally positioned to do something about it!

The healthy spiritual community prioritizes prayer, both corporate and individual. It presents petitions and supplications regularly before the Lord as a way of experiencing His peace and finding His provision. United, believers exercise their authority to bind and loose in the Kingdom of God and intercede for one another, the nation and the world. In addition, the healthy spiritual community seeks to practice the presence of God through prayers of contemplation and communion. Members learn to be still and to know Him through intimate fellowship and spiritual union.

A Celebrating Community

Although the people of the world are often hopeless and negative about life, the healthy spiritual community finds reasons to rejoice. Even in the midst of heartache, Christians know that God's love and faithfulness will see them through to victory, so they choose to praise Him. The spiritual community presents to God a sacrifice of worship through song, testimony and Scripture. As they do, the Lord draws near to bless them, and the evil one is exposed and pressed back. The central theme of each and every celebration is the wonderful, redeeming work of the Lord Jesus Christ.

In recent years many church communities have experienced significant spiritual renewal through worship. Christians have learned to lift heart and hand before the Lord as an expression of love and devotion. In response God is unleashing His empowering presence in their midst. In healthy spiritual community, worship is recognized as a commitment of utmost importance.

A Serving Community

On the night in which He was betrayed, Jesus gathered with His own spiritual community and did two things. First He celebrated the Passover, offering the cup and broken bread as symbols of His atoning death. Second, He took towel and basin and washed the disciples' feet. In both cases the Lord demonstrated sacrificial service, calling the community of believers to go and do likewise.

A healthy spiritual community is committed to service, not only to one another but beyond itself to the surrounding world. Its members extend the love of Jesus selflessly through ministries of compassion and caring. Following the example of Jesus, the spiritual community chooses to set aside self-interest, pick up the towel and basin and serve. Such ministry flows best through humble brokenness, channels of weakness that send forth the healing, redeeming power of God's self-giving love. Blessed by the Lord, the healthy spiritual community becomes a blessing to others.

An Accountable Community

A healthy spiritual community has stated expectations of participation and holds its members accountable to them. The expectations include a commitment to each of the ingredients and covenants that enhance ongoing development and healing, including Christ-centeredness, the Spirit-filled life, grace, vulnerability, availability, prayer, celebration and service.

Accountability means that each member allows the Lord to use others in the group to encourage him or her toward wholeness. People are free to speak the truth in love and, when necessary, to confront a person when defense mechanisms are keeping that individual in some kind of bondage. The fruit of the Spirit should be evident whenever any level of encouragement and confrontation takes place. The goal is growth and freedom. Accountability strengthens the community's commitment to that end.

Conclusion

This evening as I finished writing this chapter, a member of my spiritual community called. He said he wanted to thank me for "being there when times were tough." He could not have made it through alone, he told me, and he wanted me to know how much he appreciated our friendship.

How like the heavenly Father to remind me—and, as a result, you—that this journey is not at all a private matter. It is a shared pilgrimage that demands ongoing mutual support and encouragement. No one is strong enough to make the trip alone. Those who try either turn back or become casualties along the way.

Find a spiritual director who will help guide you toward spiritual maturity. Join a healthy spiritual community in which you can grow in devotion to God and love for one another. The chilling cold of night often comes suddenly and without warning. Now is the time to find people who will help you draw near to the fire of God's faithful presence.

For Further Reading

Life Together by Dietrich Bonhoeffer
Sacrament of the Present Moment by Jean-Pierre de Caussade
No Man Is an Island by Thomas Merton
A Spiritual Formation Workbook by James Brian Smith
The Way of the Heart by Henri Nouwen

9

Your Battle Is Not against Flesh and Blood

I have been in Christian ministry too long to question the existence of Satan and evil spirits. I have experienced his barrage of lies and flaming arrows ever since declaring my faith in Christ. I have also helped countless brothers and sisters who have been harassed and derailed by his destructive schemes. While much of what he does is subtle and unnoticed, the rotten fruit of his evil work is everywhere. Whether through conflict, bondage, division, deception or doubt, Satan and his dark hoard are always at work to lure people away from God and into the destructive grip of evil.

It has been noted repeatedly that either acting as if Satan does not exist or else concentrating on him constantly are equally dangerous for the Christian. The first position allows the enemy free rein to destroy people's lives. The second leads to an unhealthy preoccupation and fear of the evil one, taking our attention from the Person of Jesus Christ and His wonderful gift of life and peace. A balanced approach to combating the evil one involves learning to stay alert and well armed against him, while continuing to grow in love and intimacy with our Lord. Scripture is the manual for everything we need to know about balanced and effective spiritual warfare.

I will *not* be addressing the topics of demonology and deliverance in this chapter. Questions like "Where did Satan and evil spirits originate?" or "Can a Christian be demon-possessed?" or "What is deliverance and how is it done?" are critical but far too extensive to cover in a single chapter. Adequate answers take time to develop and demand thorough scriptural treatment. I refer you to three books that carefully address these and other issues regarding the Christian and demonization: *The Handbook for Spiritual Warfare* by Ed Murphy (Thomas Nelson, 1992), *Demon Possession and the Christian* by C. Fred Dickason (Good News, 1989) and *Victory over Darkness* by Neil Anderson (Regal, 1990). These texts provide a more-than-adequate foundation for understanding the multidimensional issues of evil and spiritual warfare.

My concern here is to focus on how to stand firm against the powers of darkness as a fully armed and dangerous soldier of the Lord. The foundation of our discussion will be Paul's teaching on warfare in Ephesians 6. From this text I will share a biblical model for resisting the evil one and ultimately pushing him back from your life.

There is no question in my mind about the enemy's desires to get you off-course. He does not want to see you move ahead in your journey toward spiritual well-being and he is especially active during seasons of spiritual darkness, attempting to use your vulnerability to his treacherous advantage.

Consider what happened to our Lord Jesus. Following an incredible encounter with the heavenly Father at His baptism, Jesus went into a lengthy period of solitude, prayer and fasting. The Bible tells us He went into the desert—a wilderness stretching over an area of 35 by 15 miles. It is a place the Old Testament refers to as *Jeshimmon*, which means "the devastation." Crumbling limestone, dust heaps and jagged rocks mark the landscape of this shimmering blast furnace. Jesus went into the desert in preparation for His journey to the cross. In the wilderness the evil one came to Him at His weakest and most vulnerable point with one goal in mind: He wanted to lure Jesus into a subtle yet devastating compromise of the will of God.

What Satan attempted to do to our Lord, his evil cohorts try on us. As we journey through our own dark night, let us be well armed and watchful. Peter warned that "the devil prowls around like a roaring lion looking for someone to devour" (1 Peter 5:8). The testimony of experience tells us that unprepared Christians are wounded by his attacks. Let us learn, therefore, to stand against him in the power of our Lord Jesus Christ.

The Victory Is Ours

Having sounded a warning against the devil's real and dangerous schemes, I want to encourage you with the good news of Christ's victory. The Bible tells us clearly and emphatically that the evil one is a defeated foe. Jesus Christ has won over all the powers of darkness, and He did it for you. The battle is real but the victory is completely and eternally yours. You are not a helpless victim of the devil but an overcoming victor with Christ. Jesus has made every necessary provision for your daily life, including the power and means to resist evil. If you are mature in your understanding of spiritual warfare and careful to walk in the light of God's Word, you have nothing to fear. Again, *you have absolutely nothing to fear.*

Meditate on the following promises and instructions that come from Scripture:

> God made you alive with Christ. He forgave us all our
> sins, having canceled the written code, with its regula-

tions, that was against us and that stood opposed to us; he took it away, nailing it to the cross. And having disarmed the powers and authorities, he made a public spectacle of them, triumphing over them by the cross.

Colossians 2:13–15

. . . He too shared in their humanity so that by his death he might destroy him who holds the power of death—that is, the devil.

Hebrews 2:14

You, dear children, are from God and have overcome [evil spirits], because the one who is in you is greater than the one who is in the world.

1 John 4:4

The Lord is faithful, and he will strengthen and protect you from the evil one.

2 Thessalonians 3:3

The Lord will rescue me [Paul] from every evil attack and will bring me safely to his heavenly kingdom. To him be glory for ever and ever. Amen.

2 Timothy 4:18

Confidence and hope should pour into your heart in light of the truths you have just read! The testimony of Scripture is full of such passages, assuring you that His strong arm is mighty to save. Be serious about the battle but never fearful. The Lord Jesus Christ has made a way for your victory, promising that God "will soon crush Satan under your feet" (Romans 16:20).

Fully Armed and Dangerous

There is no reason for Christians to stand naked and defenseless against the onslaught of Satan. But many believers do, even offering the enemy opportunities to harm them at very close range. Lack of awareness of God's provision and living in disobedience are certain invitations to disaster. Sin gives the devil critical ground in his fight against us, and a person unarmed, even if out of ignorance, offers him a vital, defense-free target.

Don't be so naïve and ill-prepared! Scripture calls you to stand against Satan's strategies, fully armed with divinely empowered weapons that enable you to defend yourself (see 2 Corinthians 10:4).

Paul's teaching on spiritual warfare in Ephesians 6 is one of the best-known teachings in Scripture, and perhaps the most important scriptural teaching we have on the topic of spiritual warfare. Throughout the history of the Church, Christians have turned there for help against the attacks of Satan. This passage is central to any discussion of the conflict between evil and the Christian. It offers practical insight and advice on how to stand strong during difficult times. I go over the essentials of Paul's instructions every single day during prayer. I would not consider moving out in life and ministry without doing what this section of God's Word says.

Let's divide our discussion of this critical passage according to four themes:

1. The nature of the battle we face
2. Putting on the armor of God
3. Being constant in prayer
4. Learning to be alert

The instructions from the Lord, through the apostle Paul, will help you recognize and overcome the enemy's deceptive and often vicious attacks. They will keep you moving forward on the journey to spiritual maturity, despite the obstacles and barriers the evil one brings your way.

The Nature of the Battle We Face

Kelly Atkins was saved out of a lifestyle of alcohol and drug abuse. He was 32 when he gave his life to the Lord following a long stay in a drug rehabilitation program. Kelly was led to Jesus by one of his caregivers in the treatment center, who plugged Kelly into a local church with an aggressive discipleship program for ex-offenders. It was just what Kelly needed.

Eight years after his conversion, Kelly had grown into a solid follower of Christ. He held down a good job, had a nice wife and served the Lord through a wide variety of ministries. In countless ways Kelly was a miraculous example of the transforming power of Christ. That is, except for one recurring problem.

For eight years Kelly had fallen back routinely into a pattern of drug and alcohol abuse. It happened about twice a year, usually around the same seasons. All seemed well and then, for no apparent reason, Kelly began to drink and ended up intoxicated or high for several days. Always penitent, he picked himself up and moved on again in Christ. Then, five or six months later, he fell again. It was almost a predictable cycle. Christians would pray, he would make new commitments and everything would seem fine—for about six months.

Finally Kelly went for professional help. The root of his problems was multifaceted. Emotional issues needed serious attention—wounds of the past left unaddressed far too long. There was also a physical component. A doctor diagnosed Kelly with a chemical imbalance that caused mood swings, a problem for which he needed medical treatment. His abuse had been an effort to self-medicate his problem. Then there was a sin issue in his life rooted in a lifetime of rebellion. But also, and very importantly, there was ongoing spiritual warfare. A significant part of the battle was Satan attacking Kelly's weakness and oppressing him into destructive behavior. Ongoing freedom involved being armed against the evil one. Psychology and medicine were not enough. The battle included a spiritual dimension—a dimension that too often we do not consider.

Paul urges believers to "be strong in the Lord and in his mighty power" (Ephesians 6:10). Why? Because the worst part of our battle in life is far beyond our ability to handle. It is the war waged in the spiritual realm— the war that affects our world in many ways every single day. Paul wrote:

> Our struggle is not against flesh and blood, but against the rulers, against the authorities, against the powers of this dark world and against the spiritual forces of evil in the heavenly realms.
>
> Ephesians 6:12

Too many Christians have an unbiblical worldview that downplays the activity of the supernatural in our midst. Paul did not share this opinion. He taught that spiritual forces are all around and, given the opportunity, work against our lives. The Bible teaches, moreover, that some "effects" we experience find their origin in the supernatural realm. In other words, not every illness, argument or accident is the result of a natural cause. Some are the work of evil spirits, and no pill or conversation or workman's tool can help.

In his *Handbook for Spiritual Warfare*, Ed Murphy comments that our battle in life includes cosmic forces of evil and dark principalities. He concludes from the teachings of Paul that believers face "a complex spiritual army—a hierarchy of evil supernatural beings who have thoroughly infiltrated the heavens and exercise great control over the earth."[1]

The word *struggle,* Murphy points out, is from the Greek word *pale,* which means "wrestle." It is a term used only this one time in Scripture, taken from the Greek world of sports. Murphy quotes Dr. Kenneth Wuest, who writes that this term refers to a

> contest between two in which each endeavors to throw the other. . . . When we consider that the loser in a Greek wrestling contest had his eyes gouged out with resulting blindness for the rest of his days, we can form some conception of the Ephesian Greeks' reaction to Paul's illustration. The Christian wrestling against the powers of darkness is no less desperate and fateful.[2]

In his choice of images and words, Paul does not undermine the seriousness of the battle we face. The forces of darkness are too powerful for mere human strength. Standing against evil demands the power of God actively moving in and through your life. This power is yours by faith in Christ Jesus. Given the nature of the difficult journey of life, you *must* know how to access this divine endowment.

There is no doubt that our problems, like Kelly's, are often multidimensional in nature. We may need emotional healing, and possibly even medication and a physician's care at times. But do not be deceived into thinking that is all our struggles involve. Since Christians wrestle against the forces of darkness, Paul teaches us how to stand in the evil day. He encourages us first to put on the armor of God.

Putting on the Armor of God

In Ephesians 6:13 Paul writes:

> Therefore put on the full armor of God, so that when the day of evil comes, you may be able to stand your ground, and after you have done everything, to stand.

Notice several introductory observations about this verse. First, the armor does us no good sitting in the closet. It is effective as an offensive and defensive weapon only when you put it on. Second, you must wear the full armor, every piece, or else you leave yourself wide open in one or more areas of your life. Third, you do not put it on just when the forces of evil threaten. You wear it constantly, fully prepared for the unsuspected evil day.

Obviously Paul is speaking figuratively about armor as we know it. Each piece symbolizes a specific and critical work or provision of God, made available to every believer. Declaring those promises and truths by the prayer of faith arms you against the strategies of the evil one. Every day, as I said, I pray on each weapon by faith, claiming the divine provision for my protection throughout the day.

The Belt of Truth

Historians tell us that the Roman soldier wore a kind of skirt made of clothlike material. This article of clothing was cumbersome and quite restrictive. As such, in the time of battle a soldier tucked this skirt into a belt around his waist, freeing his legs for unrestricted movement. Then nothing could encumber his moving forward, regardless of the pace of battle.

The primary tactic of the evil one is deception, getting us to question what God has declared true. Putting on the belt of truth means we are ready to move forward in the power of the Gospel. It is a declaration that Jesus has overcome the evil one and that we are victors in and through Him. We also are people choosing to live according to the promises of that Gospel, aligning our beliefs and actions according to its eternal principles and precepts.

The Breastplate of Righteousness

The soldier's breastplate was to cover his chest and abdomen against the blows of an enemy. It protected the vital organs which, if hit, would bring certain death. The breastplate of righteousness is based not on our right living, but on the righteousness given us by Christ. It is the powerful declaration that, in Christ, we have been given a new nature and identity that perfectly reflect the Lord's character and glory. This righteousness is not earned or deserved; it is a gift of God's grace to every believer.

As the evil one presses his attack with shaming, condemning, demeaning accusations, stand firm in the knowledge that you are a new creation in Christ Jesus. The Lord has made a way for you to be the beloved son or daughter of the Most High, with the full rights and privileges of that nobility. This endowed righteousness has divine power to guard your heart from the debilitating blows of Satan that attempt to hammer you with feelings of worthlessness and guilt. You are now safely covered for life in the beautiful righteousness of Jesus Christ.

The Gospel Shoes of Peace

Shoes are critical to the soldier called to move forward over very tough terrain. Battle is no time to be slowed by jagged rocks or painful blisters. Victory lies out in front of the soldier and he must be able to cover ground quickly on the way toward the enemy. So our feet, Paul teaches us, are covered with Gospel shoes of peace. I believe he is telling us that the equipped spiritual soldier does not lose his footing in battle because he is at peace with God.

Earlier in the letter to the Ephesians, Paul emphasized that before Christ we were at enmity with God, far away from His presence because of sin. But through the blood of Christ we have been drawn close to God and are now eternally at peace with Him (see Ephesians 2:12–13). But how many times I have believed the enemy's lies that told me God was angry with me, disappointed and distant!

Armed with the Gospel shoes of peace, I am confident that He loves me, delights in me and longs to be intimate with me. Declaring this truth causes me to run forward in life, not cower back in fear. Because of Jesus Christ, you are at peace with God, and that peace is powerful in the day of evil.

The Helmet of Salvation

The helmet had two purposes in battle. The obvious use was protecting the head against fatal wounds. A blow to the head would render a soldier defenseless and open the way to sure defeat. So it is in spiritual battle. An attack against an unprotected mind is the enemy's first strategy in assaulting God's people. Roman helmets were also often adorned with insignias and symbols of previous victories. These served as powerful reminders of how the soldiers had overcome in former battles. The symbols signaled to the enemy that these were not green troops but seasoned warriors with a history of past victory.

I believe Paul is showing you how to move forward against the mind games of the evil one. You must guard your mind by declaring repeatedly the past victory of Christ. The foe is defeated and sentenced to eternal fire and punishment. You must trust this truth no matter what the evil one tries to tell you. Also, your helmet should instill hope in your life. Regardless of the difficulty, in Christ you can overcome in the evil day.

The Shield of Faith

Ed Murphy provides valuable insight into warfare once again by describing the nature and use of the soldier's shield:

> The round shield of the early legionnaires had long since been elongated; two thirds covered his body and one third covered his comrade to the left. This brilliant innovation encouraged tight ranks, since each fighter was in part dependent on his neighbor for protection.[3]

Using this image, Paul tells us that the shield of faith is our defense against the flaming arrows of the evil one. As Satan launches his barrage of destructive lies, harassments, oppression and affliction, Christians stand shoulder to shoulder declaring their faith in the power of Jesus Christ. Our shield extinguishes every arrow as we sing, speak, shout and pray out, "Greater is He that is in me!" If asked, the Holy Spirit will empower your faith, helping you move forward even when evil fire is filling the air, threatening destruction and defeat.

The Sword of the Spirit

The well-trained soldier is skilled at close combat, using a razor-sharp sword as his weapon of choice. The sword is used when the battle is fierce and right upon the warrior. Using this metaphor, Paul teaches us that it is the Holy Spirit who empowers the believer's use of the sword, which is the Word of God. The Spirit, not you, makes the sword effective and efficient in time of battle. He infuses dynamic divine power into the truths that best defeat the enemy in the moment of battle.

The sword of God's Word is, in this case, the inspired sayings that specifically counter the evil lies and accusations of Satan. The Greek use of the term *rhema*, for *word*, identifies the sword as particular promises that are yours through the ministry of Christ's death on the cross. As the enemy comes in close at hand to destroy you with, for example, threats of condemnation, the Holy Spirit will bring to your mind the truth that "there now is no condemnation for those who are in Christ Jesus" (Romans 8:1). You can then make this declaration against Satan as a powerful, razor-sharp sword.

Far from defenseless, you can approach each day fully armed for battle. By praying on the armor of God, you enter the day with the weapons necessary to stand against the schemes and strategies of the evil one and his forces of darkness.

You have not yet fully entered the necessary strength of the Lord, though. Paul insists that you move now to the ministry of continuous prayer.

Being Constant in Prayer

Ever since becoming a Christian, I have heard it said that prayer changes things. I must tell you that this maxim is only partly true. By personal experience I have learned that faithless, selfish, fleshly prayer is absolutely worthless! It changes nothing and, in fact, can make a situation worse because it gives birth to disappointment in our hearts. If you want to be a truly effective prayer warrior, you must learn to pray with faith in the authority of Jesus Christ and stay submitted to the power of the Holy Spirit. Even the youngest Christian can move mountains when this kind of prayer is lifted before the heavenly Father!

The apostle Paul tells the Ephesians that prayer is an essential ingredient in combating the evil one. Since evil spirits operate in the heavenlies, you must do battle against them there. Your access to this spiritual realm comes through prayer. Paul instructs believers to "pray in the Spirit on all occasions" (Ephesians 6:18). I will refer to this from here on as *warfare prayer* in order to remind you that the specific context of this admonition is spiritual battle against forces of darkness aligned against you. Warfare prayer enables you to do violence against the enemy in a way that truly changes things.

Two Ingredients of Warfare Prayer

Before we look at five kinds of warfare prayer that should be part of our warfare arsenal, let's first discuss its two essential ingredients.

FAITH IN CHRIST'S AUTHORITY

Imagine for a moment that living next door to you is a nest of drug dealers violating your neighborhood. Suppose that one day you decide to go over and clear them out by arresting every one of them. You walk up to the door, knock politely, and a vicious, hate-filled dealer shouts, "What do you want?" You respond, "I'm here to arrest you. Everyone come out with your hands up, so I can tie you up and take you to the police."

What do you think would happen? Would he say meekly, "O.K., I'll get everyone out here"? If he did not take your head off right there, he would probably move into your face and say, "Who do you think you are?" What he would mean is, "By what authority do you do this, and do you have the power to back up your order?" Seeing that you have neither power nor authority behind you, he might just kill you for bothering him.

Now imagine the same scenario, but instead you are a well-armed policeman in uniform backed by one hundred heavily armed officers and agents. Everything changes, doesn't it? The drug dealer has a decision to make: *Do I go peaceably or let them carry me out after they loose their firepower against us?*

On our own we are nothing against the forces of darkness. Weak, faithless, naïve prayers do nothing—or, worse, they anger the evil one and trigger an all-out assault against us. You remember what happened to the seven sons of Sceva when they did this (Acts 19:14–16). It was not pretty. But if you engage in true warfare prayer, the balance of power swings overwhelmingly to your side.

The first element of warfare prayer, then, is faith in the authority that is yours in Jesus Christ. We already discussed the victory that Jesus won over the enemy. That victory is yours and it has placed you in a position of authority over the forces of darkness. That's right! You, by faith in the Person and work of Christ, are an officially recognized authority with grace-given rights over evil spirits.

Most Christians are not aware of this, and as a result live under the spirits' tyranny. But when you pray against evil spiritual power, the weight of the government of Jesus Christ stands behind your requests.

In Ephesians 1:20–23 Paul wrote that Jesus is now seated at the right hand of God in heaven, above every rule, authority, power, dominion and title now and forever. Everything, absolutely everything, is under His feet. But that is not all. Paul tells us that you and I are "seated . . . with him in the heavenly realms" (Ephesians 2:6). This means that, by grace, the Lord has allowed us to assume His position of authority. And when we pray in harmony with His reign and rule, we move forward with Kingdom rights over the forces of darkness.

In other words, you can speak on His behalf. Your word of rebuke becomes His word. This is the authority of true warfare praying. It must be exercised humbly before God, in complete honor and harmony with Jesus

Christ. It is not a toy and must not be used in a cavalier manner. But you can move out boldly to stop the enemy with full faith and confidence in the Lord.

Faith in the Power of the Holy Spirit

The second element in warfare prayer is power. Going back to our earlier illustration, one policeman does have the authority to arrest ten drug lords. But does he have the power? One hundred officers and agents back in the police station do him no good in the moment of crisis. He needs their power right there with him when he knocks on the door to make the arrests.

The power in warfare prayer is the active, overwhelming presence of the Holy Spirit. His work (as we detailed in chapter 3) makes the dynamic difference in the Christian life. When you submit to His ministry in and through your life, things happen. Without Him your prayers of authority lack the power necessary to accomplish the task. Jesus gave His disciples authority to reach the world on the day of His ascension, but He told them to do nothing until the Holy Spirit came to fill their lives. Why? Because He is the necessary power behind the authority. Before Pentecost the disciples, while full of authority, were fearful followers of Christ behind locked doors. After Pentecost they were bold witnesses of Christ who spilled out into the streets with supernatural gifts and power.

Moving against the enemy in the power of the Holy Spirit means several things. First, you must be filled with His presence for daily living. Moment by moment you need to choose to submit to His leading, teaching, cleansing and power. Time and again every day I cry out, "Holy Spirit, take over. Help me reckon my life as dead at the cross. Live the life of Christ through me in every way." The seed of this prayer must grow to become a tree—the ruling principle in your life.

Then, praying in the Spirit means your prayers are initiated by the Spirit Himself within you. They pour out of His presence in your life, stirred by His initiative. The Holy Spirit must shape your prayers, guiding you in the specific requests and petitions you lift before the Lord. The Spirit delivers the prayers in that His presence in your life is what connects you to the heart of God the Father. And the Holy Spirit empowers your prayers, giving them the force necessary to accomplish the work of the Kingdom.

Praying in the Spirit takes on a dimension that is noticeably different from normal prayer. You sense a new power and effectiveness. Spirit-filled prayer is the way you should always pray "on all occasions" (Ephesians 6:18). All effective prayer must be initiated, shaped, developed and empowered by the Holy Spirit.

Warfare prayer offered in authority and power changes people and circumstances. Although the battle is real, the victory in Jesus Christ is assured. But Paul does not end his comments about prayer there. He adds that you and I must pray "with all kinds of prayers and requests" (Ephesians 6:18). What does he mean? Broadly we may define this as every different kind of prayer taught or modeled in Scripture.

I would like to highlight a few kinds of prayers that should definitely be part of our warfare arsenal.

United Prayer

While each individual believer holds power against the evil one, there is a dynamic increase of strength when we unite in prayer, and a dramatic increase in the combat power aimed against the enemy. In the Old Testament we read that God's people united could rout an army. Moses said that two Israelites joined in battle could "put ten thousand to flight" (Deuteronomy 32:30). United prayer joins faith to faith, bringing increased courage in the face of battle. In difficult times call your brothers and sisters to your side and go to your knees and fight!

Agreeing Prayer

Jesus told His disciples that "if two of you on earth agree about anything you ask for, it will be done for you by my Father in heaven" (Matthew 18:19). Jesus was explaining that believers in agreement have the power to bind and loose on both heaven and earth. Agreement invites the presence of Christ into the context of prayer, taking the potential of our prayers to a new level. Agreement means harmony, unity and shared union among the people involved. It also means the individuals are united around a joint request, claiming a common promise of God's provision for the moment. Agreement provides a united and irresistible front against the forces of darkness.

Persevering Prayer

In warfare prayer, never give up until the break-through comes. Recall Jesus' parable about the man who needed bread from his friend (see Luke 11:5–8). When he went to him late at night to make his request, the friend told him it was an inconvenient time to meet his need. But the man persevered until finally his friend gave him the bread. Jesus told His followers to be like that in prayer. Sometimes the oppressive power of evil is not pressed back instantly. But continue persistently to make your request known, trusting the Lord's ultimate victory. Many people miss their promised provision simply because they give up too soon.

Intercessory Prayer

Warfare prayer is not limited to our own issues. There are times the Lord burdens us with problems others are facing. When they are overwhelmed or at risk, He calls us to intercede for them in prayer. This is a ministry of great privilege, for it models the very ministry of Jesus on our behalf. The Bible says "he always lives to intercede" for us before God (Hebrews 7:25). We are called to stand in the gap for our brothers and sisters in much the same way. In my darkest night, people interceded on my behalf and I know it helped me profoundly in the battle.

As a prayer warrior you can affect events in people's lives around the world. Sending missiles of warfare prayer is one of the most important ministries of the Kingdom. In fact, you do well to know that anything accomplished on earth is probably accomplished first in the heavenly realms by an intercessor.

The Prayer of Praise

Praise is a powerful weapon against the enemy. Nearly a decade ago I wrote a book on worship entitled *Exalt Him* in which I discussed the need for Christians to join in worship as an intentional act of warfare against Satan. In the face of his violent schemes, we must unite our voices in declarations of honor, glory and adoration. Praise is a warfare weapon we need! Since writing that book I have received letters in which people tell me that "worship warfare" made a difference. Churches have gathered to praise in combating illness, divorce, job loss, rebellion, poverty and racism. Praise releases the glory of God so brightly that the darkness must flee or be absolutely destroyed.

"[Praying] in the Spirit on all occasions with all kinds of prayers and requests" (Ephesians 6:18) changes things! Learning the dynamics of warfare prayer is invaluable to your daily life and ministry, and you will progress more successfully along the journey through difficult times when you are well familiar with this powerful weapon. Adding warfare prayer to the armor of God changes you from an old footsoldier into a nuclear threat!

But you are not done with your training. Paul adds one last element to your battle stance: learning to stay alert.

Learning to Be Alert

Any soldier who fails to stay alert in enemy territory invites disaster for himself and his comrades. And we are most definitely living in enemy territory!

> We know that anyone born of God does not continue to sin; the one who was born of God keeps him safe, and the evil one cannot harm him. We know that we are children of God, and that the whole world is under the control of the evil one.
>
> 1 John 5:18–19

Since you and I are in Christ, we are not of this world but awaiting transport to our final destination. Our ministry is to reconcile others to God so that they, too, might enjoy heavenly citizenship. But right now everything and everyone of this world is under the control of evil powers. This is where the evil one does his work, and as soldiers we must always be watchful. Pray regularly for discernment. Ask the Holy Spirit to sensitize you to the presence of evil so that you can defend yourself and rescue others.

But in some ways this seems unpleasant and unwise. Isn't it better not to know? On the other hand, if a rattlesnake were slithering on your bedroom floor, wouldn't you want to know? I think you get the point. The Holy Spirit can signal you, by quickening your spirit, when evil is present. Things may appear perfectly in order, but inside you sense the presence of evil. This will help you

185

stand alert and even smoke out the enemy before he can do his deceptive work.

You also need to spot the ways of the enemy. The Bible uses various metaphors for the evil one as ways of identifying his activities. Several of these images include:

- *The ruler of this world* (1 John 5:18–19). Satan works through the governmental and societal structures of this world to do violence to the Kingdom of God. The result: political oppression and persecution of every kind.
- *The prince of the power of the air* (Ephesians 2:2, KJV). There is a spiritual hierarchy of demon powers that seek to harass, deceive and destroy people. Though unseen, they are ever active and always present under the ultimate authority of Satan himself.
- *An angel of light* (2 Corinthians 11:14). The evil one often appears in good, religious ways, even presenting a very moral presence. The truth is, he uses the appearance of light to draw people into ultimate dark. Cults are an obvious example, but various extremes of legalism and Pentecostalism may also reflect his schemes.
- *A roaring lion* (1 Peter 5:8). Satan hurls threats of destruction, hoping to isolate believers from God's flock so he can devour them. It is critical that we maintain unity against evil, standing shoulder to shoulder and close to God.
- *Slanderer* (1 Timothy 5:14). Evil spirits love to capitalize on our proclivity for gossip by igniting controversy through slander, rumor and suspicion. Many fine Christians have been damaged because weaker believers fell prey to this familiar tactic.
- *Accuser* (Revelation 12:10). Jesus Christ has forgiven you and me of every wrong, every sin, every

failure. Yet Satan tries to get us to feel condemned, worthless and guilty before God. These feelings never originate with God. The enemy knows that getting us to doubt God's unconditional love leads to self-destructive behavior.

Satan has been defeated but remains very active, and he will be until the end of history as we know it. But you can stand strong in the evil day. Jesus has made every necessary provision for your protection and victory. Your part involves taking hold, by faith, of the powerful warfare weapons He has made available. With joy and confidence in Him, arm yourself daily with the armor of God, and take up the position of prayer that enables you to push back the forces of darkness. Then, diligent along the way, you can journey toward freedom convinced of the Lord's care and increasingly consumed in Him.

For Further Reading

The Handbook for Spiritual Warfare by Ed Murphy
The Bondage Breaker by Neil Anderson
Mighty, Prevailing Prayer by Wesley Duewel
The Prayer Shield by C. Peter Wagner
Christianity with Power by Charles H. Kraft

10

Praising God in the Valley Unleashes His Power

Getting away for a week alone with my wife sounded like a good idea. My doctor had suggested we stay at his cottage for some much-needed rest and rebuilding. I had been battling depression for almost two months and was tired and frustrated. It did not seem that much was changing, so maybe time away would help. Tom's summer home was high in the Sierra Nevada mountains, located on a beautiful lake. The setting was picturesque and the view magnificent. Since going there was what the doctor ordered, I would give it a try.

Cheryl and I left the children with my parents and spent a week together there, hoping to regain strength for the battle. Our time consisted primarily of light conversation, long walks and plenty of rest. Each evening we listened to music, read Scripture and prayed together. The dark cloud was ever present, but I did begin to feel a bit of hope that somehow things would turn a corner.

After a few days we called home to check in and were glad to learn all was well. Then my mother said I had received a call from Ray Larson, who wanted me, if possible, to telephone him. I knew Ray by reputation only.

He was the senior pastor of a large congregation in our community. The church numbered more than two thousand and was well respected by Christians and non-Christians alike. My interest piqued, I made the call.

Ray was gracious, asking about my health and promising ongoing prayer support. Then he told me the Lord had impressed him to call, specifically to have me read 2 Chronicles 20. There was a very important message in this passage for me, he said, and it would be key to moving forward through this dark night. Ray emphasized that the key was praising the Lord in the midst of the battle.

I thanked him sincerely for his concern and assured Ray I would meditate on the text. After a pleasant exchange of thank yous, I hung up. But my immediate reaction to the call was not particularly good. In fact, I was almost angry.

"Praise the Lord? Is he kidding me? I haven't had a pleasant thought in weeks, am constantly hopeless and in tears, and feel that life is virtually meaningless. And this guy wants me to praise the Lord? He doesn't even have a clue. I don't feel like praising the Lord. I feel like crying until I have no more tears to shed."

I am sure that if you have ever walked through a season of difficulty and trial, you can relate to my reaction. "Praise the Lord, anyway" is often little more than a religious cliché offered by people who often do not really know how to help, or who live in perpetual denial. It can be a syrupy, superficial solution offered by insensitive people for life-threatening pain and loss.

In a way I wanted to believe this was the situation with Ray, but deep inside I knew better. He is known as a man who hears from God. Beneath my anger and skepticism I sensed that there was something here from the Lord. So I turned to 2 Chronicles 20 and began to read.

The children of Israel were being threatened by the Ammonites and Moabites. The enemy army was large, strong and on the move toward God's people. King Jehoshaphat was frightened, so he and the people went to the Lord in fasting and prayer. God responded to their cry and spoke words of comfort through Jahaziel:

> "This is what the LORD says to you: 'Do not be afraid or discouraged because of this vast army. For the battle is not yours, but God's. Tomorrow march down against them. . . . You will not have to fight this battle. Take up your positions; stand firm and see the deliverance the LORD will give you.'"
>
> verses 15–17

So Jehoshaphat appointed men to lead the army, singing praises to the Lord for His splendor and holiness. They sang of God's constant care, declaring that He would love them forever. Then the Bible says:

> As they began to sing and praise, the Lord set ambushes against the men of Ammon and Moab and Mount Seir who were invading Judah, and they were defeated.
>
> verse 22

God so confused the enemy that they turned and annihilated one another! Then Jehoshaphat led his people into the valley, where it took them three days to carry off all the plunder. God not only defeated their enemy but blessed the Israelites with the spoils of war. In the end the people of the Lord renamed the battlefield the Valley of Beracah, which means "The Place of Praise."

This story from 2 Chronicles hit me hard. The Lord was clearly speaking to me and the analogy was right on. I was facing a great battle against an overwhelming foe, and he was assaulting me in a time of intense darkness. But if I chose to praise the Lord, trusting His love, I would be able to draw near to the fire of His presence. There I would more than win. He would enable me to see the enemy coming and to stand victorious in the glory of His protection. I realized it was not an issue of feelings but a choice of the will.

And so I turned to the Lord in prayer. I confessed my feelings of weakness, asking the Holy Spirit to strengthen me for the task. Then I committed myself to grow strong through praise as an offering of obedience before the Lord.

It would be nice to tell you that the cloud lifted immediately. It did not. But I mark that day as a turning point in the battle. Choosing praise made a critical difference, turning my position from a defensive to an offensive strategy. God's power became increasingly obvious, and as I turned my heart toward Him, He lifted His hand against the enemies of my life. Praise changed the battleground to a spiritual plane, and the Lord's power was too much for the evil one. As a result, I am still carrying off the spoils of battle from our own Valley of Beracah. The most important treasure has been a new understanding of praise. It is a multidimensional priority of Kingdom living that not only blesses the God who is worthy, but opens His storehouse to those who make praise a way of life.

People who find themselves in unexpected times of trial and suffering will be glad they discovered the gift of praise.

The Priority of Praise

Praise must become the preoccupation of your life. Scripture is clear on this point: Praise is an aspect of your very calling as a child of God. Consider the following passages as a sampling of God's Word instructing you to choose praise as a way of life:

> You are a chosen people, a royal priesthood, a holy nation, a people belonging to God, that you may declare the praises of him who called you out of darkness into his wonderful light.
>
> 1 Peter 2:9

> Through Jesus, therefore, let us continually offer to God a sacrifice of praise—the fruit of lips that confess his name.
>
> Hebrews 13:15

> Praise the LORD.
> Praise the LORD, O my soul.
> I will praise the LORD all my life;
> I will sing praise to my God as long as I live.
>
> Psalm 146:1–2

> Praise the LORD.
> Praise God in his sanctuary;
> praise him in his mighty heavens. . .
> Let everything that has breath praise the LORD.
> Praise the LORD.
>
> Psalm 150:1, 6

We can see that all through the Bible, by example and command, praise is to characterize our love and devotion to God. It is a right and proper response to the wonder and majesty of God's nature and redeeming acts.

British pastor Derek Prime ably speaks in the introduction of *Created to Praise* of the priority of praise in the believer's life:

> I wanted to try to establish the right position of praise in the Christian life, because praise occupies a unique

place in God's purposes. When God first formed man, man was created to praise God; when we are born again, through faith in our Lord Jesus Christ, we are recreated in order that we may praise God.

We must not be afraid to express the depths of our feelings as we worship God. If we raise our voices in praise and welcome of some important state dignitary, should we not raise our voices at the presence of the King of kings and Lord of lords? Even as there is variation in tempo and volume in a beautiful piece of music, so there will be variation in the expression of our praise to God. What is important is that we should not be inhibited in expressing sincere praise. . . . There is no danger of our being over-enthusiastic in our praise of God if it is from our heart. The soul that is in love with Jesus Christ must sing! What are our lame praises in comparison to His love?[1]

Prime goes on to emphasize that praise should be the believer's companion throughout life, whether through peace and prosperity or trial and sorrow. Praise is the privilege and responsibility of all of us. We must seek to grow in our understanding and practice of praise, learning to embrace its various expressions as a sacrifice before the Lord. As we do, we will discover that it releases an unbelievable response of power and provision from the Lord. While always important, praise is especially vital along the pilgrimage through hardship and trial.

Why Praise the Lord?

Have you ever done something but did not really understand why? Maybe you saw everyone else doing it, knew it was right and simply joined in with them. For many Christians praise is like that. They know it is important and sense inside that it is part of following

193

the Lord. They see and hear people praising God in church and prayer meetings and eventually do it, too. But no one ever took the time to explain what it is really all about.

In this case, ignorance is not bliss. I believe understanding the principles of praise ignites a person to invest even more in its practice. I once read a book entitled *There's Dynamite in Praise*. In its fullest expression, that is exactly how powerful praise can be to the Christian. It has the potential to unleash the presence of God, to fight back the evil one and to transform a person's attitude in even the darkest of times. We do well to embrace praise as a lifestyle, reorienting our perspective on the ups and downs of life.

What follows is a discussion aimed at answering, at least in part, the question "Why praise the Lord?"

Praise God Because He Is Worthy

It is important to understand that the foundational motivation to praise is not self-centered but God-centered. Praising God is based on who He is and what He is like, regardless of your personal circumstances. Your life situation—good or bad, blessing or curse—in no way affects the praiseworthiness of almighty God. This does not mean denying or suppressing your own dark feelings and negative emotions. You are not only free but encouraged to express every thought, need and concern before the Lord in prayer. (Even a casual reading of the Psalms, as we saw in chapter 6, tells us this.) But the basis of praise does not depend on your own issues. It is purely a matter of God's glorious being, no matter what you are experiencing at the time.

Consider the traditional definition of the word *praise*. It means, according to *Webster's New World Dictionary*, "to set a price or value, to declare worth, to laud, glory, approve or admire." You can see that the activity of praise does not depend on the condition or circumstance of the person praising, but exclusively on the nature and character of the object being praised.

So you must engage willingly in the activity of praise purely because of the value, worthiness and glory of God. Even before you consider the Lord's incredible redemptive work on your behalf, there is an eternity's worth of reasons to praise Him. And Scripture gives you the insight into His nature that sets your adoration and admiration into motion.

Over the years I have used a prayer outline to help me be consistent in intercession. Wanting to begin with worship and adoration, I went to the Bible and collected a list of the revealed characteristics of the Lord. I spend time every day contemplating each attribute as a prelude to praise. The list includes the facts that God is

Holy	Sovereign
Loving	Infinite
Benevolent	Eternal
Gracious	Omnipotent
Merciful	Omnipresent
Patient	Just
Faithful	Righteous
Omniscient	Compassionate
True	

You can get delightfully lost in any one of these immutable attributes of the Lord! Each aspect of His nature is unfathomable in depth and expanse. Praising Him for any of these traits gets the focus of attention entirely off of yourself and onto the wonder of the living God. This is vitally important in tough times because praise battles against narcissistic introspection.

Although there are secondary benefits to this kind of worship—such as instilling in you renewed trust and confidence in the Lord—the goal is adoring the God of glory. Praise Him because He is supremely worthy, wonderful and, quite frankly, beyond description. His praise-worthiness stands true when the bottom falls out from under you. As you enter trial and difficulty, remain in the position of praise.

There is no better model than the prophet Habakkuk. At a time of great oppression and incredible loss, he expressed his confidence in the majesty of God:

> Though the fig tree does not bud and there are no grapes on the vines, though the olive crop fails and the fields produce no food, though there are no sheep in the pen and no cattle in the stalls, yet I will rejoice in the LORD, I will be joyful in God my Savior.
>
> Habakkuk 3:17

Why praise? Habakkuk gives us the first part of the answer: Because of who God is—no matter what your lot personally—and because of His glory. Whether you feel like it or not, praise is a response to God that you cannot afford *not* to make. Silence the noise of your troubled thoughts and burdened emotions, enter His presence by the Spirit and offer the sacrifice of praise He deserves.

Granted, it may take time to unload the baggage of your circumstances. But when you choose to persevere in praise, the moment comes when your spirit becomes present before Him. Adoration betraying description will draw you into a mystical union illumined by the light of His glorious life. With the prophet of old and the adoring throng surrounding God's throne, you will cry, "Holy, holy, holy is the Lord God Almighty" (Revelation 4:8).

This is the foundation of praise that even now awaits your participation.

Praise God because of His Mighty Acts

No matter what else happens in your life, you must not make the mistake the children of Israel did. They kept forgetting the mighty acts of God and neglecting to praise Him for His provision and intervention. Busy with life, they allowed their hearts to stray from the Lord, failing to stop and worship Him. Not only was this a sign of gross ingratitude, but it set the stage for future disaster. Forgetting to recount God's power and previous deliverances, the Israelites responded to crises with fear and unfaithfulness. They became the victims of dark times through which they would have gone victoriously had they stayed their posts in the position of praise.

If you fail to worship the Lord for His mighty and wondrous acts of power and deliverance, your fate will be the same.

On one occasion of great celebration for the nation of Israel, David wrote a magnificent psalm of praise and thanksgiving. In it he called the people to consider the many miraculous acts of God and respond with songs and shouts of adoration:

> Give thanks to the LORD, call on his name;
>   make known among the nations what he has done.
> Sing to him, sing praise to him;
>   tell of all his wonderful acts.
> Glory in his holy name;
>   let the hearts of those who seek the LORD rejoice.
> Look to the LORD and his strength;
>   seek his face always.
> Remember the wonders he has done,
>   his miracles, and the judgments he pronounced. . . .
>
> Ascribe to the LORD, O families of nations,
>   ascribe to the LORD glory and strength,
>   ascribe to the LORD the glory due his name.

> Bring an offering and come before him;
> worship the LORD in the splendor of his holiness.
>
> 1 Chronicles 16:8–12, 28–29

David called the people to remember what God had done for them, to praise Him for His mighty acts, wonderful miracles and the provision of His ongoing strength. David's example provides a valuable model for our own lives. Why praise? Because of all God has done in the glory of creation, in the work of redemption and in His ministry of daily deliverance and provision for His children.

Drawing from David's example, we can see three categories of God's mighty acts for which we praise Him.

ACTS OF CREATION

Do you want a place to start your praise? Just ask the Holy Spirit to illumine your heart and mind to the magnificence, wonder and joy of creation. When He opens your eyes even slightly, you will respond with a torrent of adoration and delight. The works of God are breathtaking in their detail, expanse, variety, complexity and function. From the magnificence of space to the wonder of the microscopic, our universe is a miraculous display of the handiwork of God. All of it, every mysterious reality, exists in response to God's creative word. The sages of all time have only scratched the surface of understanding what our Lord spoke into existence. His divine imprint is all around, able to draw you into indescribable seasons of praise.

I have a friend with a brilliant, scientific mind whose insights into astronomy, physics, biology and ornithology are, to my lay understanding, amazing. Gary approaches the world around him with childlike wonder and delight, and behind every discovery seems to learn more about God. Once I listened in awe as Gary described the process of pollination in various types of orchids found in the South Pacific. I was enraptured, not only with the interesting details but with Gary's genuine joy and excitement in it all. In the end he said, "Isn't God fantastic?" From that moment on I prayed that I would no longer walk through life with blinders on. I asked the Lord to illumine my own heart and mind to the glory of His creation so resplendent with the fingerprints of His divine touch.

Once David was so caught up in the glory of creation that he wrote these words:

> The heavens declare the glory of God;
>   the skies proclaim the work of his hands.
> Day after day they pour forth speech;
>   night after night they display knowledge.
> There is no speech or language
>   where their voice is not heard.
> Their voice goes out into all the earth,
>   their words to the ends of the world.
>   Psalm 19:1–4

David's words can serve as a wonderful introduction to your own song of adoration. Let your voice resound with heartfelt praise to the God of glory, who placed you in a panoramic theater that continuously displays the wonder of His power and might.

ACTS OF REDEMPTION

For what other reason should you embrace a lifestyle of praise? Because of the unbelievable works of redemption God has performed lovingly and faithfully on your behalf. How do you even start praising God for His mighty acts of salvation? They are as numerous as the stars and reach back in history to the fall of Adam and Eve. He could have abandoned you in your own private hell, justified to turn His back on you forever. But out of a love that transcends definition, the Lord worked out an intricate plan of redemption that cost Him everything, then offered it to you as the most undeserved gift on record.

The content of your praise could go all the way back to the calling of Abram and include every redemptive act recorded in salvation history. The longest season of praise centers on the Person and work of the Lord Jesus Christ. His life, ministry and death are the greatest and most central part of God's redemptive plan. Words, songs and testimonies of the Lord's work of salvation should flow from your heart. You need but consider the various truths of His incarnation, death and resurrection for praise to erupt from within you.

Whether you focus on God's love, which gave Jesus as payment for sin, or His Son's willingness to lay down His precious life on your behalf, a sacrifice of praise is the only right and acceptable response. An eternity of worship will barely begin to express the gratitude and devotion that should be yours. Then add to this the treasure of blessings that come to the redeemed. The Lord's ministry to the lost actually defies description.

The content of God's redemptive acts does not end even there. Go on to include every detail of your personal salvation story. The specific events of your redemption bear testimony to the faithfulness of God. How you came to hear the Gospel, the context of your turning to Him, the changes that occurred in your life—all are part of the testimony of God's mission to redeem your life. He has done great and marvelous things to give you a place at His side, and for each one, you do well to lift a sincere and sacrificial offering of praise.

ACTS OF DELIVERANCE AND PROVISION

God did not rescue you from the bondage and destructive garbage of the Fall, clean you up and then say,

"You're on your own now." No, He stays with you to make sure you have all you need. Whether daily provision for life, help in fulfilling your mission or strength against the forces of evil, God keeps with you all the way. He even goes so far as to place His Holy Spirit within you as Comforter and Helper, Teacher and Guide. If walking through a storm of life is best for you, He offers you His strength for the journey. When direct intervention is needed, the Lord will spare no means, angelic or miraculous, to provide for your needs and deliver you from the destructive power of evil.

Jesus told His disciples not to worry about the issues of life. He assured them that God knew precisely what each of them needed, and when. "Look at the birds of the air," He instructed them, and, "See how the lilies of the field grow" (Matthew 6:26, 28). Both exemplify His love and care. Jesus assured His followers that they were worth far more than the birds or lilies to the heavenly Father. "Seek first his kingdom and his righteousness" He said (verse 33), and God will do the rest.

God's mighty acts of deliverance and provision should do two things for you. First, they give you reason to praise His glorious name. Thanks and adoration should spill out of your life, overflowing from a heart of ceaseless gratitude. Second, His acts of the past should bring you hope and confidence in the day of trial and darkness. He came through before and He will again. Let praise empower you to relax in the trust of faith and wait for His loving hand of deliverance.

Praise God Because It Unleashes His Presence

While teaching at Alliance Theological Seminary, I was concerned for the students' spiritual well-being, which can be at risk during the difficult days of academic life. So, with the help of a friend, I began a Saturday evening service of praise. The format was simple. We gathered to worship, give testimonies and share briefly from God's Word. Seven people came to our first service. It was a small beginning. But within a year, the Saturday evening praise-and-prayer service grew to an average of nearly two hundred. In time faculty members and staff made it a regular part of their schedules. Even people from the community joined in.

What was the attraction? Unquestionably the sense of the presence of God that blessed each service. Whenever those students began to praise the Lord, He began to move in a tangible and observable way. The Holy Spirit would come and bless us all. Seasons of renewal and refreshing were a regular part of the experience. Praise unloosed the power of God, and every one of us soaked in His presence. Services designed to last an hour often went on late into the evening. Seminary students found new strength for their studies, renewed passion for the Lord and a refreshing sense of joy about them. Praise opened the way.

Several years later I had the privilege of watching Risen King Community Church grow from seven people to nearly one thousand. The major factor responsible for that growth: the presence of God released during the worship service. From the very beginning our congregation determined that worship would be top priority. People were led and instructed in the dynamics of praise as a pathway to God. As a result, the Lord blessed us consistently with His presence, where people have been gloriously and consistently changed.

Praise ushers us into the throne room of the Almighty, where He gloriously touches our lives. The renewal occurring through worship around the world today is happening precisely because of this principle. Whether at corporate gatherings or in private moments, the Lord is responding faithfully to the praises of His people.

King David knew well the relationship between praise and the presence of God. He spoke of God being enthroned in praise (see Psalm 22:3). Some scholars translate this as God "inhabiting" praise, but the point is the same. David recognized the relationship between worship and experiencing God's power and provision.

In 1 Chronicles 13 and 15 we read that David wanted the Ark of the Covenant—the tangible representation of God's presence in Israel—near him in Jerusalem. The king apparently wanted God's help and provision right with him at the center of his government. So he arranged for the transport of the Ark from the home of Obed-Edom. David went to great lengths, after an earlier fiasco, to move the Ark properly, and he surrounded the event with a major celebration of praise, using singers, musicians, priests and ongoing animal sacrifices. Then, overtaken with praise, David danced before the Ark as it entered Jerusalem. God's presence was moving, and adoration and worship led the way.

You, too, should hunger and thirst for the presence of God in your life. He alone can set you free from the bondage of sin, push back the forces of darkness and strengthen you for all that life brings. In His presence you can see problems for what they really are—steppingstones to personal growth, opportunities for His healing and helping touch. God's presence is a place of love that brings acceptance, and a place of holiness that will humble you as you draw near.

The journey I am on would do me in if I could not be renewed regularly at His throne and soak in His presence. Practically this means two important things. I gather weekly with other believers for corporate worship and praise. Together we lift our hearts in adoration, declaring His glory and ascribing God the worth due His name. Second, I make praise a daily part of my life. Through psalm reading, prayers of praise, various acts of worship and music, I enter His presence. Often I sing along with worship albums, engaging my whole heart in celebration of His nature, redemption and deliverance. Such praise helps me draw near to the God who is always present.

You and I were created to enjoy and draw strength from God's presence. Praise from sincere and humble hearts opens the floodgates of His power. Make praise a regular part of your journey through the valleys of life.

Praise God Because It Pushes Back the Evil One

The evil one looks for every possibility to deceive and destroy our lives. He and his demon hoard are determined to harass, oppress, afflict and enslave us, and they seek every opportunity to work their wicked schemes. God's Word calls us to be watchful, aware of their relentless efforts to do us harm. Yes, the enemy has been defeated at the cross and sentenced to eternal fire. But until his demise, he is working furious malice against the children of God.

If you have followed Christ for any time at all, you know that life includes spiritual warfare. The struggle, as Paul said, is not against flesh and blood but against evil principalities and powers (see Ephesians 6:12). This seems especially real in seasons of trial, when the evil one concentrates his efforts to destroy your faith. The battle is real, as we saw in the last chapter, and should never be taken lightly. It is essential that you use every available weapon to protect yourself and push back the forces of darkness.

In this chapter I want to emphasize the relationship between praise and spiritual warfare. The Bible gives specific instructions regarding the place of praise in times of battle. Symbolically the story of Jehoshaphat and the Valley of Beracah teaches us that praise routs the enemies of the Lord. As we lift up words, songs and shouts of adoration to the Lord, His power is released and the evil one is defeated. Praise is like an intense beam of light blinding the forces of darkness. When the evil one moves in against you, begin to sing and speak words of truth about God's love, power and the provision that is yours in Jesus Christ. As you do this, the enemy will flee.

Cathy Hoyer is a dear friend who often receives prophetic insight from God through dreams. One night she dreamed of a great army of demons coming against her across a barren plain. She was being enveloped by hideous beings of darkness threatening her annihilation. Then Cathy heard the Lord calling her to lift up her voice and hands before Him in praise and adoration. As she did, a beam of light came from above, reflected off her hands and blinded the evil spirits, sending them in retreat. When Cathy awoke, she had a new and powerful understanding of the relationship between praise and spiritual warfare—an understanding that will help us, too.

Consider what the following passage of Scripture teaches us about praise and spiritual conflict. The psalmist writes that even a child can resist the evil one by the power of praise: "From the lips of children and infants you have ordained praise because of your enemies, to silence the foe and the avenger" (Psalm 8:2). What amazing power God gives through praise! If even a child declares the truth of God's majesty, wonder and mighty acts, the threats of the enemy are silenced. Given Satan's constant barrage against God's children, praise should become a way of life.

Another psalm teaches us that praise is a companion to the sword in time of battle:

> May the praise of God be in their mouths
> and a double-edged sword in their hands,

> to inflict vengeance on the nations
>   and punishment on the peoples,
> to bind their kings with fetters,
>   their nobles with shackles of iron,
> to carry out the sentence written against them.
>
> Psalm 149:6–9

Since God's Word is "sharper than any double-edged sword" (Hebrews 4:12), I believe the Lord is telling us that Scripture and praise are mighty weapons against the evil principalities and powers that harass us. Use them together and the forces of darkness will be defeated, even shackled in fetters of iron. Praise inflicts painful punishment on them. How exciting to think that your positive declarations of truth bless your own life and defeat the powers of darkness at the same time!

There also seems to be a clear relationship between worship music and praise. I have often used recorded music to help me press through periods of oppression and harassment. Joyful, celebratory songs and hymns of the Lord serve as weapons of punishment, sending demonic powers running. Isaiah spoke of this when he said:

> Every stroke the Lord lays on them with his punishing rod will be to the music of tambourines and harps, as he fights them in battle with the blows of his arm.
>
> Isaiah 30:32

Praise will lift your heart and spirit into the place of joyful fellowship with God. At the same time, worship music punishes the dark forces seeking to level their voices against you.

It would take an entire book for me to tell about God's deliverance brought about through praise. Time after time along the pathway of my dark night, the enemy tried to work his evil schemes against me. At times he caught me unguarded, and the blows of deception pummeled me. Often, because I failed to be watchful, I handed him an opportunity to knock me down. But praise in the name of Jesus Christ always pushed him back. Whether it was at my initiative or that of my wife or friends, declaring the glory of God ignited His presence and the evil one had to flee.

You cannot afford *not* to praise. Learn its every dimension and practice it as often as you take a breath. Praise is a response to the glory of God and has Kingdom power and potential for your life. No matter how bright the day or dark the night, the journey will never yield its treasures unless you commit to live a life of praise.

Some Practical Suggestions

Let's take another look at Hebrews 13:15, since it provides us with a key admonition: "Through Jesus, therefore, let us continually offer to God a sacrifice of praise—the fruit of lips that confess his name."

First we can see that our approach to God is exclusively through the Person and work of Jesus Christ. He alone gives us access to the heavenly Father, especially when we come before Him with an offering of praise and worship.

Second, the writer tells us to praise continually. It is not simply to be an act or form of worship offered to God on occasion. Praise, as we have said, is to be a way of life. By the power of the Holy Spirit, set your mind and emotions and body in a position of praise, all day and every day. Granted, it takes time to embrace such an orientation to life, but embrace it you must. Praise will be your position through eternity, and practicing it now is your spiritual preparation.

Finally, notice that the author calls praise a sacrifice. This point cannot be overemphasized. My simple definition of sacrifice is "a willing presentation of something of value, given joyfully from a sincere and pure heart." In this case praise is the sacrifice and God the One to whom you make your presentation.

I suggest that your "sacrifice of praise" include the following.[2]

Make a Sacrifice of Your Words

Lift up your voice continually with words of praise and adoration. When you are alone, direct your words to God, focusing on every aspect of His character, His mighty acts of creation, redemption and deliverance. When you are with other people, your praise can be both focused toward God and directed toward them as a testimony to His goodness and matchless grace.

Your sacrifice of praise can include the spoken word, using various passages of Scripture and personal phrases of praise; words in song, whether hymns, spiritual songs or choruses of worship; and, when appropriate, shouts before the Lord, such as the oft-repeated biblical declaration "The Lord reigns!"

Make a Sacrifice of Your Body

Body language is recognized as a powerful form of communication. It can represent the attitude of the heart and the proper response to the presence of God in our midst. Biblically we find admonitions to kneel, to bow low or to lie prostrate before the Lord. Each of these acts symbolizes various aspects of reverence, submission and humility as we enter God's presence. The Bible also encourages us to clap, which I believe symbolizes hearts filled with delight and wonder at the nature and goodness of our heavenly Father. Various psalms encourage us to lift hands in praise, which represents surrender—a desire for intimate embrace and the position of need and dependence. The Bible also gives examples of dance as an appropriate response to God's presence.

In each case the symbol is to be an outward expression of the heart. We do well to include such acts in our private praise, and, when appropriate, join other believers in integrating them into times of worship and celebration. These acts of praise are not to be fleshly displays of self-righteousness but Spirit-filled acts of humble praise, offered in love to God.

Make a Sacrifice of Your Possessions

You and I place some degree of value on our goods and money. Since they have worth to us, they qualify as acceptable sacrifices before the Lord. Our praise, therefore, should include acts of offering in which we present our possessions before the Lord as an act of worship. Such an expression of praise represents the full and total giving over of our lives to the Lord.

Giving a sacrifice of our possessions is also a response to God's total self-giving at Calvary. His sacrifice moves us to sacrifice. Because He gave, we give. A sacrifice of possessions is an act of praise that symbolizes our thanks, trust and desire to participate in the ministry of God's Kingdom. A sacrifice of possessions also breaks the spirit of greed and self-sufficiency that permeates our society. It releases the blessing of God on our lives as we let go of what we own in order to lay hold of the One who is our all in all.

I know full well that it is not easy in the valley. Times can be hard as you journey across the tough terrain, and it is very possible to lose heart. When you do, the ground beneath you becomes an impassable bog of hopelessness and despair. You can become so weak that giving up seems your only recourse. At that moment the lies of the evil one come at you like a firestorm of flaming arrows. What can you do to keep the course and break through spiritual weakness to renewed vitality?

Learn to praise the Lord, and give yourself to it as a way of life!

For Further Reading

A Celebration of Praise by Dick Eastman
The Hallelujah Factor by Jack Taylor
Worship His Majesty by Jack Hayford
31 Days of Praise by Ruth Myers
A Knowledge of the Holy by A. W. Tozer

Spiritual Disciplines Move You toward Christlikeness

What is the Christian life all about? Throughout this book I have likened it to a journey that leads you at times through very difficult places. But where is this journey ultimately taking you?

I realize most of us think of our final destination as heaven, but is that the end toward which we are moving along in life? Is the sum total of Christianity escape from eternal fire by entering everlasting paradise? This is a dimension of our pilgrimage through life, but does entering our heavenly home signal the completion of our lifetime pilgrimage of faith?

I propose that the journey's end is far more glorious than even our indescribable eternal home. Rather than moving through life simply to find a place of everlasting rest, we are on a lifelong pilgrimage toward eternal harmony with God.

This was, in fact, the pre-Fall relationship Adam and Eve had with God in Eden. That wonderful spiritual union was what made the Garden paradise. Yes, it was a place of magnificent delights far beyond anything we know today. But the place alone did not hold the power ultimately to fulfill Adam and Eve's lives. It was the pure and perfect union that offered our first parents all they could ever want or need.

Our Christian journey is moving us once again toward such a realized harmony. We exiles of Eden are, through the redemptive work of Jesus Christ, on a pilgrimage of ascent.

Allowing the circumstances of life to shape you spiritually is a critical part of your journey toward harmony with God. Yes, Jesus has given you His perfect righteousness so that you stand before God as a perfectly holy son or daughter. But there remains a daily working out of that saintly status so that you walk experientially in the same union with God that Jesus had. As you allow the Holy Spirit access to sanctify your life, you move closer and closer to that glorious destination of union. And if God so graces you, moments of that indescribable harmony are possible even on earth. Saints throughout history have spoken of such experiences with God in terms that make everything else in life pale in comparison.

But the sad fact is, most of us accept a far less consuming relationship with God. We do this partly out of ignorance, because we do not know there is more. Or we choose less because we are well aware that moving on costs everything. Harmony may be a gift of grace, but laying hold of it demands our all. We still do not believe the teaching of Jesus that to truly find life, we must die. Harmony, or union with God, demands the crucifixion of self. And that death is not easy, so many satisfy themselves in this life with less. But for those who say, "God, do it in me," the Father provides glimmers of our ultimate destination that motivate us to move on. He is the treasure and pearl for which we give all to obtain.

Five Levels of Relationship

I have contemplated five different relationships available between God and humankind. The degree to which we allow Him to work in our lives determines the level of relationship we can experience. Note, as I say that, that He does the work and we respond. No striving or self-effort determines our experience of intimacy with the Father. Closeness and moments of union come, like all else in the Christian life, by grace. But unleashing that work is related to your willingness to surrender, which involves the continuous death of self.

Following are the levels of relationship you can have with the heavenly Father. These definitions are obviously not categorical, but a way to understand your pilgrimage as a Christian man or woman, and a backdrop to the discussion in the rest of this chapter.

Unaware of God

This category represents people who have not been regenerated spiritually through faith in Jesus Christ. They may or may not believe in God or be religious. But inside they are spiritually dead and eternally lost. I refer to them as unaware of God because they have no personal experience of His presence within and they are unable to have even the remotest harmony with the heavenly Father.

Born in God

This phrase refers to people who have accepted the redemptive work of Jesus Christ as their own, and through the Holy Spirit have been regenerated to new spiritual life. God has placed His Holy Spirit with them, providing the possibility of ongoing fellowship and help. Like newborn babies, these people have all they need for true harmony with their heavenly Father. They are spiritually immature, however, needing continued development toward healthy Christian living. Innumerable Christians stay in this stage their entire lives, missing out on the dynamic relationship with God that is possible in Christ.

Doing for God

People in this stage have come to understand that the Christian life involves service to the purposes of the Kingdom. To one degree or another they have responded to the call to ministry (perhaps vocational servants, but not necessarily). These people know that evangelizing the world, helping and caring for the broken, and serving brothers and sisters are elements of true discipleship. Most likely people in this stage have a working understanding of spiritual gifts.

This level represents many in the evangelical church— a mighty force for Kingdom good in the world. The downside is that far too many think doing for God is the centerpiece of the Christian life, and they run the terrible risk of not growing in intimacy with the heavenly Father.

Filled with God

In the past quarter of a century, countless Christians have begun to cry out once again, "There must be more than this!" Every generation comes to this point, it seems, wanting more than knowledge of God. Hungry for an experience of His living presence, they begin to pray for genuine spiritual life and vitality. They ask for an outpouring of His presence to ignite them with renewed passion. The modern charismatic renewal is an example of such a movement. People in this stage open up to a new level of dependence on the Holy Spirit. Tired of trying in their own fleshly power, they seek to walk out the Christian life filled with His power. What results are new effectiveness in service and experiences of God's presence in times of prayer and worship.

As exciting as this is, there is a downside as well. Experiences of God's presence and power can be sought for reasons other than genuine harmony with Him. People can desire Holy Spirit infilling in order to be more productive in service or to feel the awesome power of His presence—while union is still to come.

Living in God

This phrase represents, for me, the ultimate destination of the Christian life. It signifies union, or spiritual harmony, and will be our eternal experience beyond this life. In this stage, if we are surrendered to the process of dying to self, moments of selfless oneness are possible. By God's grace we can be so caught up in Him that nothing else matters, or even appeals to us, but union with the heavenly Father.

The concept of union with God is not common among evangelical Christians. Although it has been used by Catholic spiritual directors for centuries, Protestant believers are unfamiliar, and in some cases uncomfortable, with the phrase. They are concerned that it may suggest a nirvana-like experience in which an individual loses all self-awareness and is absorbed into the consciousness of God.

That is not what is meant, nor does "union with God" suggest a godlike status or some kind of escapist experience one can find in the next life. Union with God, as I mean it, refers to the truth that a Christian can move to a place of spiritual maturity in which "I no longer live, but Christ lives in me" (Galatians 2:20). It is allowing the Holy Spirit to bring about the death of the self life so that we are yielded fully to the presence, purpose and purity of God's will.

One author described this stage by saying that a person is "caught up in rapturous joy, adoration, praise and a deep peace that passes all understanding."[1] It is what Jeanne Guyon referred to as "abandonment unto God," in which personal desires and appetites in the moment

215

no longer exist. Only God, and what is of Him and for Him, matters. In union, people rest in the awareness that they no longer live in and for themselves. True life is total absorption in Him. In such moments, eternal or otherwise, nothing matters but God.

Four Components of Spiritual Formation

Jesus Christ our Lord lived in perfect union with His heavenly Father. He told His followers that He and the Father were one. When Philip asked to see the Father, Jesus replied that "anyone who has seen me has seen the Father" (John 14:9). Jesus said repeatedly that He came to do only the Father's will and that He could, in fact, do only the things He saw the Father doing (see John 5:19). The Lord lived in spiritual harmony and union with God as no one did before Him. And not a single person was able to do the same after Jesus, unless he or she learned how to do it through Him.

The bottom line question is simply this: Is it really possible to experience union with God? Can you realize this destination even for a moment? Or is it so far out of our grasp that it is an impossibility until heaven? How can anyone but Jesus know this harmony?

The answer is simple: Anyone who is like Jesus can experience what Jesus experienced. And, to put even more definition to the journey we have been discussing, the Christian life is a pilgrimage toward spiritual harmony and union with God as we grow increasingly Christlike in our nature, attitudes, appetites and actions. If we surrender to this purpose, everything we experience and do can be used by God to bring about this end in our lives.

For centuries Christian mystics used a term for this process of transformation. They called it *spiritual formation*. The very best working definition of this phrase is provided, I believe, by Dr. Robert Mulholland in his book *Invitation to a Journey: A Road Map for Spiritual Formation*. He defines spiritual formation as "a process of being conformed to the image of Jesus Christ for the sake of others."[2]

Mulholland's definition has had a great impact on my understanding of spiritual formation. It helped me see that the Christian life involves ongoing transformation toward Christlikeness. Every day in every way, you and I have the opportunity to surrender to that glorious yet often painful process. We do it because it draws us even closer to the relationship with the heavenly Father that our Lord Jesus modeled. Right now, if we are willing, you and I are being shaped for spiritual union with God.

Let's return to that definition of spiritual formation. In *Invitation to a Journey,* Dr. Mulholland divides his definition into four components that shed light on the multidimensional nature of Christian spiritual formation. I want to unfold the meaning of each dimension in a much briefer way here, so that we can better understand our pilgrimage toward Christlikeness.

Process

The first element of spiritual formation is that it is a process. To be honest, in many ways I wish Christian maturity came as the result of one big spiritual blast. My saying this should identify me as a baby boomer thoroughly influenced by our cultural preoccupation with instant gratification. In our home we have an instant-on television, instant breakfast food and instant access to the information highway. I carry a card that provides me with instant cash at the automatic teller machine, and I live in a society where getting something right now is hardly soon enough.

This widely accepted attitude has affected our understanding of spirituality. Many of us are looking for that one moment of spiritual ecstasy that will catapult us beyond day-to-day difficulties. But this is not God's way. Your heavenly Father moves on your life over the course of time. Yes, certain crises can move you forward with sudden surges of growth, resulting in new spiritual vitality. But on the whole, spiritual development is a process. It involves seasons of movement that vary in speed, as well as times of rest and waiting. Sometimes the process affects your life noticeably. At other times it seems that nothing at all is happening, and you may wonder what is wrong. There are seasons of difficulty and others of abundance. There are periods when spiritual activity is intense and other times when life appears mundane. Yet all along the way you are being transformed—if you are surrendered—to the image of Jesus Christ.

I say *if you are surrendered* because you can choose against what the Father is doing. When you do, however, you are actually deciding to become more and more enslaved to darkness. Robert Mulholland is crystal clear on this point. The process, he emphasizes, is happening whether you like it or not. Everyday decisions, trials, relationships and events come your way that you cannot stop. But if you react to what comes in unhealthy ways, it shapes you into something other than the image of the Lord Jesus Christ. Mulholland writes:

> Spiritual formation is not an option. The inescapable conclusion is that life itself is a process of spiritual development. The only choice we have is whether that growth moves us toward wholeness in Christ or toward an increasingly dehumanized and destructive mode of being.[3]

God works in the process to shape you into a healthy spiritual man or woman. But you must actively surrender and choose, time and again, to orient your life to His transforming activity.

Being Conformed

For as long as I can remember, I have been a person of constant activity. My wife complains lovingly that my foot shakes back and forth even in my sleep. Restless within, I have spent much of my life looking for something to do. Once I identify it, I tend to put my head down and not look up until I finish the job. I have spent more than four decades as a type-A workaholic.

On becoming a Christian, I wanted to know what I had to do in order to grow. As well-meaning yet misinformed Christians spelled out do's and don'ts, I went right at the task—and did not look up until I was flat on my back in a horrible dark night.

During those difficult days I learned that my spiritual development is not my job; it is God's. My role is simply to surrender, over and again, to what He is doing. Formation is not about my performance or striving. It is about Christ's performance and my ongoing death to self-centeredness and control. All this is to say that spiritual formation is a process of being conformed, not conforming. You and I are the ones being shaped, and the Lord is the one doing the shaping. As Jean-Pierre de Caussade emphasized, God uses everything that comes our way in the present moment.[4]

Most of us like to grab hold of the reins of life and determine the speed and direction of our journey. This, in part, is why we struggle during difficult times. We want to get out as fast as we can and hurt as little as possible. But the key to spiritual development is found in the opposite response. We are to allow God to determine speed and direction, while we respond with acts of humble trust and obedient submission. I appreciate Robert Mulholland's summary about being conformed:

> Our spiritual journey is not our setting out (by gathering information and applying it correctly to find God) (as an object "out there" to be grasped and controlled by us). It is a journey of learning to yield ourselves to God and discovering where God will take us.[5]

The Image of Christ

I have mentioned that I have a growing appreciation for the writings of the Christian mystics. There are several reasons, not the least of which is their preoccupation with Jesus Christ. They see abandonment into Him as the great privilege of life, and they instruct believers to orient all they are to that end. Saint Bonaventure, a friar of the thirteenth century, wrote a book entitled *The Tree of Life* in which he sought to unfold the wonder and beauty of the life and ministry of the Lord. He wanted his students to contemplate every dimension of "The Eternal Art," a name he used for Christ. Saint Bonaventure saw in Jesus the perfect representation of what human life is meant to represent. Contemplating Him, in Bonaventure's view, will draw believers into closer conformity with Christ. Jeanne Guyon, the seventeenth-century French mystic, wrote an entire book to help people experience the wonder of Jesus Christ.

Meditating on Christ is, as I mentioned in chapter 2, vitally important for your life. Not only does it enhance spiritual intimacy, but it enables you to see just how wonderful your Lord and Savior is in His humanity. He is the perfect expression of what God intends *you* to be like! Jesus was full of grace and wisdom, beautiful in His willingness to touch the broken and lost, self-giving to the point of giving away His very life for others. In fixing your eyes and thoughts on Him, you can see the magnificence of your Lord's nature and character, and at the same time see how very far away from His image you still are.

Spiritual formation, according to Mulholland, takes place precisely at the points of your "unlikeness."[6] You see Christ's glory and your own depravity. In the specific areas of your distorted humanity, God works to shape you into the image of Jesus. The work, as we have already noted, takes time, for the issues of your unlikeness are deep and broad. The central activity of this conforming work is death. You must allow God access, through the Holy Spirit, to all your selfish ways, so as to eliminate them from your life. He chooses the issues and the means of execution; you choose to say yes and surrender. What remains is the new, Christlike nature that was your gift from God at your conversion.

In area after area, over time and by many means, the heavenly Father shapes you to be like His blessed Son. The qualities of the Kingdom—qualities like forgiveness, love, self-giving and compassion—will begin to flow from your life as they did from the Lord's. The dynamics of the journey are there for a divine purpose—that you be like Him and come to enjoy spiritual harmony with the Father, as He did on earth and does this day in glory.

For the Sake of Others

Henri Nouwen, in his book *Life of the Beloved,* teaches us that every Christian is the "beloved" of God, just as Jesus Christ was.[7] Nouwen argues that, as "the beloved," you and I are called to live for God in the world, as Jesus did. Using the Lord's action at the Last Supper as an illustration, Nouwen says that we all are taken by God, blessed, broken and then given away to the world. This was the experience of Christ's life and it is to be your way as well.

Let's look at each of these elements.

To be taken signifies your chosenness, in which you are specifically called by God to be His son or daughter. It is an act of privilege based exclusively on grace. *To be blessed* means that God endows your life with every spiritual blessing you will ever need. He lovingly opens the storehouses of heaven for your well-being. *To be broken* is the fate of every human being, including God's children. But rather than react to your weakness, offer it to God as an instrument of grace. As you do, this brokenness draws you ever deeper into harmony with the Father, and it becomes a source of help to others. As such, you are then *given away*. Looking eye to eye with the broken and rejected of the world, you are able to point them to the redeeming power of the Gospel of Christ.

This journey toward spiritual well-being is not simply for you. Like Jesus, you are to live as a sacrifice of worship to God and as a ministry to the world around you. Christlikeness means giving yourself away, for then and only then, completely empty of self, do you find true life. Evidence that you are truly growing is found not in how much you have gained, but in how much you have given away. Again, turning to Mulholland:

> If you want a good litmus test of your spiritual growth, simply examine the nature and quality of your relationships with others. Are you more loving, more compassionate, more patient, more understanding, more caring, more forgiving than you were a year ago? If you cannot answer these kinds of questions in the affirmative, and, especially if others cannot answer them in the affirmative about you, then you need to carefully examine the nature of your spiritual life and growth.[8]

Spiritual formation is the process of being conformed to the image of Christ for the sake of others. This process, which occurs every moment of every day, is preparing you to reach your destination: spiritual union and harmony with God. You will never know or understand purpose and fulfillment in life until you experience that blessed union. And it is impossible to experience harmony with the Father apart from being like Jesus in every way. You will not be shaped into His glorious image unless you say yes to the process. Regardless of the ups and downs and difficulties of the journey, you must yield to the Father's conforming hand. As you do, you will move on to the high call of God.

Spiritual Disciplines

Is there something you can do to enhance the process of spiritual formation? Are there specific actions and commitments that will draw you close to the transforming fire of God's presence? If you remember that the shaping is God's work, the answer is yes. There *are* things you can offer your heavenly Father that will enable Him to bring you closer to His purifying flame. Begin to work spiritual disciplines into your life.

There was a time when I responded negatively to the concept of spiritual disciplines. *Oh no,* I would think. *Not another talk about having a devotional life!* My workaholic past had almost completely burned me out on "devotions." This was because I saw the disciplines as yet another task I had to complete in order to become a good Christian. That notion is off course and, in the long run, counterproductive.

Spiritual disciplines are activities we embrace that give room for God to work in our lives. These activities have been proven channels of His grace throughout history—places where the Father has chosen to manifest His life-changing touch. Remember, the work is His. It is His choice to bless or not bless what you offer Him. The discipline is not effective in and of itself. Only as God chooses to empower each means of grace can you be assured that the discipline is working in your life. When He moves through it, and how and to what degree, is completely up to Him. Your part is merely to offer the activity to Him. Your motivation: simple obedience and love.

Earlier I encouraged you to regularly contemplate the wonder of Jesus Christ. Doing this, I said, will shed light on how unlike Him you truly are. When you embrace spiritual disciplines, you are consciously sowing to your new, Christlike nature, in direct opposition to the sinful habits and behaviors of your old, depraved way of life. You are offering God an open channel of grace aimed at killing the flesh. It is as if you are saying, "Here, Father, use this discipline to put me to death, so that Christ can live completely in and through my life." As the heavenly Father deems best, He will.

Again let me reemphasize that all change comes from God. All you are doing is offering Him another time-tested place to do that work. The offering of disciplines must be free of conditions, such as how and when you expect God to move. That is entirely His decision. What keeps you faithful to the disciplines? Your heart of love for the Lord, which urges you to be conformed to His image.

Spiritual disciplines are effective channels of grace because they complement the principles of the Kingdom. They are activities that, in their nature, reflect the character of Jesus Christ and follow the example of His ministry. True spiritual disciplines are consistent with the fruits of the Holy Spirit and the priorities of genuine servanthood. Embracing such activities provides a proper seedbed for nurturing the ways of Christ in your life.

Before moving on to discuss the actual spiritual disciplines, I want to comment on insights provided by author Dallas Willard. His book *The Spirit of the Disciplines* is a tremendous work on the philosophical and historical background of the disciplines of spiritual formation. I am particularly challenged by Willard's comparison of the spiritual life to athletics. Many children want to enter the game, he comments, and play like their favorite athlete. They try to use the same moves and techniques that their heroes do in those clutch moments of the game. But Willard insists there is only one way a person has any chance to perform like a star athlete in the game. He or she must embrace that athlete's life of preparation before the game. Only then, when the key move is an automatic response, can the person do as the star does.[9]

What is the point? If we want to be like Jesus in the moment of decision, we must choose to live as He did every day. Jesus lived a life apart from the public, in preparation for the moment of ministry. His response to brokenness, rejection, abuse and poverty was forged in private, far from the public eye. Jesus made room for God in His life minute by minute so that His responses of healing and love came out of the overflow of that relationship.

Once again, if you intend to move toward spiritual union with the heavenly Father, you must allow God to conform you to the image of Jesus Christ. Embracing spiritual disciplines is a surrendered choice to live as Christ did, to become what Jesus was on earth and is today as the Son of God.

What Are the Disciplines?

In recent years several very helpful books have been published on spiritual disciplines. Probably the best-known work is Richard Foster's *Celebration of Discipline*. He provides a thorough, practical discussion of the nature and practice of these activities.

But I most appreciate Dallas Willard's categorization of the spiritual disciplines. He places each discipline under one of two separate headings—the disciplines of abstinence and the disciplines of engagement.

Disciplines of Abstinence

Disciplines of abstinence are activities we offer to God demanding that we abstain or give something up. These include:

Solitude: Choosing to come apart from our daily activities in order to be alone with God.

Silence: Choosing against the noise of the world and self in order to listen to the whispers of God.

Fasting: Abstaining from food for a specific period of time in order to lessen the grip our flesh has on our lives and to open the way to experience God's strength in weakness.

Frugality: Choosing, in a world of material excess, to say no to luxuries and wants, focusing on God as our satisfaction in life.

Chastity: Choosing to set aside, for a season, the sexual aspect of the marriage relationship in order to concentrate on spiritual union. Abstinence in marriage requires mutual consent.

Secrecy: Choosing to follow the admonition of Jesus to do our deeds of service and giving in private.

Sacrifice: Giving beyond our ability in response to God's self-giving and as a means to enhance trust in our lives.

Disciplines of Engagement

The disciplines of engagement are activities we embrace that build into our lives the truths of the Kingdom. Whereas the disciplines of abstinence involve giving away, the disciplines of engagement open the way for us to receive. Willard likens the difference between the two categories to "out breathing and in breathing." The first, he says, combats our sins of omission, while the second opposes our tendencies toward sins of commission.[10]

Study: Choosing to spend time meditating on God's Word. The goal of this discipline is not acquiring information but allowing God to form our lives spiritually.

Worship: Declaring the wonder and supreme worth of God and engaging our hearts, minds, souls and bodies in an ongoing offering of adoration.

Celebration: Choosing to find and experience joy in the life God gives us; celebrating the goodness of the created order in all its beauty and greatness.

Service: Engaging our lives, resources, talents and spiritual gifts in ministry to others. We accept Jesus' example of servanthood through the towel and basin.

Prayer: Communing with God through prayer and through the power of the Holy Spirit, as well as affecting the world around us and the spiritual realm through our requests and petitions.

Fellowship: Choosing to be integrated into the healthy spiritual community as a place of united strength, increased faith and demonstrated love.

Confession: Letting Jesus work through our weakness and bring us wholeness as we bring all things into the light. This discipline involves opening our broken hearts before one another for mutual strength and support.

Submission: Choosing to come under the authority and direction of those in anointed spiritual leadership. This discipline also involves seeking out spiritual directors who will help guide us toward Christlikeness.

The question I want to bring before you is this: How should you determine which disciplines to embrace, and for how long? There are two dominant factors, I am convinced, that will guide your decisions.

First, embrace those disciplines that address the areas of your weakness and rebellion most directly. The person consumed with issues of greed and power should focus on disciplines of sacrifice, secrecy, service and submission. If lusts of the flesh control your life, then fasting, confession and submission would be good places to begin. Your offering of disciplines should specifically address the issues of your unlikeness so that they might, with God's touch, bring death to the flesh.

The second consideration is prayer. As you get silent and wait on God, the Holy Spirit will lay on your heart the specific disciplines that you should embrace. His guidance is critical in that it is His power in and through the disciplines that changes your life. I have felt the Lord's direction repeatedly to specific disciplines. At times the reason was obvious, at other times not. Most recently I have felt a deep stirring for prolonged seasons of contemplative prayer, whereas previously I sensed the Lord calling me to invest more time in Scripture meditation and spiritual reading. In either case, waiting for God to direct your choice of spiritual disciplines is in itself an expression of the discipline of submission.

I recommend practicing spiritual disciplines in both solitude and community. One context influences the other, and both bring to our lives different dimensions of the same activity. Worship, for example, is a discipline that can be embraced individually or corporately. So are several others, like fasting, prayer, study, celebration, service and confession.

Many rich and wonderful insights can be gained on how to practice these disciplines. Each activity is multidimensional, able by God's power to affect your life deeply. Learning more about each one will only enhance your pilgrimage to spiritual maturity and well-being. Read the volumes listed at the end of this chapter to better understand and develop the many and varied disciplines we have discussed.

In Philippians the apostle Paul said he was confident of one thing: "that he who began a good work in you will carry it on to completion until the day of Christ Jesus" (Philippians 1:6). The heavenly Father will move on your life faithfully to conform you to the image of Jesus Christ. His purpose and process meet you daily through every circumstance, trial, relationship and task. As you surrender to His divine activity, you move even closer toward Him. While this shaping is not always easy, since it involves the death of the self life, the reward it offers is the treasure of eternal life.

May you remember that your final destination is a return to paradise, where you will be forever alive in your Father and your God.

For Further Reading

Celebration of Discipline by Richard Foster
The Spirit of the Disciplines by Dallas Willard
Invitation to a Journey by Robert Mulholland
The Way of the Heart by Henri Nouwen
The Practice of the Presence of God by Brother Lawrence

12

You Can Become a Wounded Healer

I have a vivid memory from childhood. Our family did not attend church regularly when I was small, but from time to time we made our way to a little red brick chapel in rural Venetia, Pennsylvania. It was a small country church with a sanctuary upstairs and a large, open basement where junior Sunday school was held.

It was in that basement, in a tiny class sectioned off by corkboard dividers, that I saw a picture that remains in my mind to this day. The teacher, Mrs. Green, was doing a flannelgraph lesson on Jesus' love for children. She placed colorful felt pictures of kids of all ages and races on the flannelboard. Then she reached into her folder, took out a picture of Jesus and placed it in the middle of the scene. The cutout portrayed Him in a white robe with long, brown hair to his shoulders and a tender smile. But that was not what grabbed my attention. My eyes were taken to His hands and feet. There were wounds on them—the results, Mrs. Green told us, of being nailed to a cross.

That image for me as a little boy was powerful. Although it would be years before I surrendered to Christ, the picture of the wounded Jesus stirred something deep within my soul. I was not taken aback or frightened by it. Somehow those wounds made me feel—I don't know, kind of warm and good and safe. Mrs. Green told us He received them for us.

I am middle-aged now, decades past those days in Mrs. Green's class. But whenever I think of Jesus, or whenever through my imagination I picture the Lord before me, His wounds still stand out. In fact, they are more vivid than ever, precious beyond description. His wounds are an incredible source of freedom, healing and unconditional love. Although I often weep when considering the Lord's agony at Calvary, His pierced hands, feet, side and battered brow are life to me. They are the wounds by which I am healed; they represent the suffering that sets me free.

Jesus Christ is the Wounded Healer. His broken body and shed blood are the means by which we enter the Kingdom of God. As Christians we run to the table that symbolizes our Lord's sacrifice, and there partake in and worship the Lamb once slain. His wounds neither repulse us nor cause us to stand back in horror. They invite us to draw near and be whole—a source of forgiveness and everlasting life. Yes, Jesus has wounds, and all creation responds with shouts of praise and adoration.

We, Too, Have Been Wounded

All of us have been wounded in one way or another, too. For some it is the devastation of abuse or abandonment at the hands of adults. Others are hobbled by self-inflicted injuries brought on by rebellion and bad choices. Many are the victims of destructive relationships that enslave and demoralize. The list of possibilities is almost endless, but the result is often the same.

The wounds, even when deeply hidden, seem to tear people apart.

But it is important that we face something startling about being wounded: As painful as physical, emotional or mental injury is, the real problem is not the wound itself. Rather, the long-term devastation is a result of how we handle or respond to being wounded. React to it in an unbiblical way, and sorrow and heartache result. Respond as Jesus did, in full dependence on God, extending forgiveness to the offender, and you can find unbelievable healing, not only for yourself, but also through you to others.

Choosing to Open Up

Let's consider Katherine Stark, for her life illustrates what I am trying to emphasize. We can see in her the consequences of a destructive reaction to woundedness, as well as the redemptive power of weakness when faced in and through Christ Jesus.

I met Katherine when she and her husband began attending the church I pastored. For some years I knew her only slightly. But even from that distance, I sensed that something was wrong. She worked too hard at convincing people that she had a joyful demeanor, a solid marriage and an eagerness to serve the Lord. Anyone who began to spend time around Katherine soon sensed that what she communicated was not the whole story.

The truth was, Katherine was falling apart inside, the result of her ongoing reaction to previous woundings. When she could not handle the emotional pressure anymore, Katherine risked coming to my wife and me for help.

Her sad story was all too common, the tale of childhood sexual abuse. Katherine's older brother had molested her repeatedly as a teenager—a horrible experience not easily overcome. But Katherine's nightmare continued because of her reaction to the wound.

First there was Katherine's reaction to the pain. She felt worthless because of what her brother did, and chose to silence the hurt and seek affirmation through sexual promiscuity. This offered short-term peace but led to long-term pain. Katherine also chose a way to handle her offender. She hated her brother, carrying vindictive, vengeful feelings and fantasies for years. For two decades they did not speak.

After marriage Katherine chose people-pleasing as her new painkiller. She would do almost anything for people if only they would like her. She also worked hard managing people's impressions of her. Not wanting anyone to suspect anything was wrong, she hid everything beneath a façade of bubbly happiness. While people were drawn to Katherine initially, relationships were short-lived. Her sweet shell was impenetrable and actually pushed people away.

By the time Katherine came to Cheryl and me, she was experiencing serious emotional upheaval. We referred her to a support group especially sensitive to her issues. We also began to encourage Katherine to deal with her wounds in the strength of Christ. Over time she grieved her losses before the Lord, extended genuine forgiveness to her brother and, by faith, received deep emotional healing.

Finally—and here is where the subject of this chapter comes in—Katherine moved on to open up about her wounds, offering them to the Lord as a source of healing to others. Instead of hiding, Katherine began to tell her story to illustrate Christ's healing power. She did not make her wounds her identity or a badge of honor. She simply allowed her weakness to become the vehicle of Christ's strength. As a result she has a growing ministry to other victims of sexual abuse. Whereas once people were uncomfortable with Katherine because of her dysfunctional reactions to woundedness, now they find in her a pathway to wholeness. Katherine Stark is a wounded healer, a living example of Christ's power made perfect in weakness.

Christ's Strength through Our Weakness

I have seen this grand reversal dozens of times in recent years. In fact, the most powerful servants of God I know are men and women who have been deeply wounded, yet are dearly and decently vulnerable and weak before others. While many still suffer, they have ceased trying to manage their pain and people's reactions to them. Instead they stand surrendered before the cross, allowing the healing power of His wounds to flow to and through their own wounds.

Consider the powerful ministry of Larry Crabb. His insights into mental and emotional trauma are profound, and Crabb is recognized globally as a leader in biblical counseling. But by his own admission, Crabb has seen his ministry affected by his own struggles with the dark night. In the introduction to *Finding God* he writes:

> Let me tell you why I wrote this book. I have come to a place in my life where I need to know God better or I won't make it. Life at times has a way of throwing me into such blinding confusion and severe pain that I lose all hope. Joy is gone. Nothing encourages me. . . . I wrote this book in response to the desperate cry of my heart to know God better.[1]

This is the testimony of a wounded healer, a man struggling openly with his own pain as a context for offering Christ's healing to others.

Andy Comiskey has an equally powerful ministry of healing for people struggling with homosexuality. Andy is founder and director of Desert Stream Ministries, aimed at helping the sexually dysfunctional find freedom in Christ. His book *Pursuing Sexual Wholeness: How Jesus Heals the Homosexual* offers help and hope to those caught in the gay lifestyle.

Comiskey, a husband and father, is a very effective teacher and widely sought-after speaker. But it is his own testimony of Christ's ability to heal the homosexual that marks Andy's ministry. Jesus met Andy in that very weakness, calling him to repentance and obedience. In that struggle he encountered the strength of the living Lord. Now Andy's wounds are the channel of Christ's healing to others.

The names of wounded healers are endless—people like Robert McGee, Joni Eareckson-Tada, Henri Nouwen, Charles Colson and Gordon MacDonald. They have learned that the object of great pain can become the source of blessing when surrendered to Christ. For them, pretending or putting on a pretty face is of no value. What counts is the strength of Christ Jesus made perfect in the weakness of frail, suffering human beings who find healing in His wounds. These men and women humbly offer their own wounds in turn as a context for His ministry to other broken men and women. When treated like this, personal wounds do not offend; they attract people straight to the Lord.

This format for ministry leaves little room for personal pride. It is humbling to have people see you in all your weakness. It used to be, when I was introduced as a conference speaker, that the focus was on my education, achievements or other acceptable qualifications. I was Terry Wardle the doctor, professor, author or church planter. No one ever asked me about woundedness, weakness, brokenness or suffering. It made me feel better about myself. It felt fulfilling and safe.

But now I have a new ministry that grew out of being crushed, exposed and scrutinized as "a man who had a breakdown." No longer am I sought out as a church growth expert or denominational leader. Instead people turn to me in the context of my failure, my dark night and my ongoing weakness—and there find the strength of Christ.

It was difficult at first. Initially I wanted to avoid any conversation about what I had gone through. It hurt to talk about it, and I was afraid that dialogue might cause me to revisit some very scary places. But soon I realized that Jesus was present in those moments of ministry, touching others powerfully through my own pain. In fact, I met Him there more dynamically than in any other place of service. So I have grown to cherish weakness because He is present to strengthen and to heal. I no longer want to hide what happened. Instead I have offered my wounds to Him as a channel of His grace to other broken people. And when someone is helped, it is not about me; it is about Jesus.

The apostle Paul wrote about this principle in his second letter to the Corinthian church. Under the inspiration of the Holy Spirit, Paul urged believers to find Christ's strength in the midst of weakness. Illustrating from his own life, he declared confidently that the grace of God is all the broken and battered need to turn wounds into opportunities for Kingdom growth. I most appreciate Eugene Peterson's paraphrase of that text:

> Because of the extravagance of [my] revelations, and so I wouldn't get a big head, I was given the gift of a handicap to keep me in constant touch with my limitations. Satan's angel did his best to get me down; what he in fact did was push me to my knees. No danger then of

walking around high and mighty! At first I didn't think of it as a gift, and begged God to remove it. Three times I did that, and then he told me,

"My grace is enough; it's all you need.
My strength comes into its own in your weakness."

Once I heard that, I was glad to let it happen. I quit focusing on the handicap and began appreciating the gift. It was a case of Christ's strength moving in on my weakness. Now I take limitations in stride, and with good cheer, these limitations that cut me down to size—abuse, accidents, opposition, bad breaks. I just let Christ take over! And so the weaker I get, the stronger I become.

2 Corinthians 12:7–10, TM

Openness within the Local Church

Every local church carries the potential for effective Kingdom ministry. But it will not be born out of some well-designed program or canned approach to doing the work of God. Instead these ministries are linked to the weakness of each and every member of the local church. Behind every face is a story of woundedness that can, if approached biblically, be the avenue of healing and hope to others. The man hiding his sexual addiction can, when freed in Christ, point others to the Savior who bears our sexual sin. The woman who has struggled privately with debilitating fear can find in Christ a peace that passes understanding, and then allow her story to be the vehicle of help to countless others. On and on the examples go, with limitless possibilities. Wounded healers can be freed and equipped to touch people where they live, ministering more powerfully in weakness than they ever could in pretentious strength.

Yet, as thrilling as this appears, serious changes must be made within most of our churches if this potential is to be realized. We have bought into the notion that appearance is more important than reality. Brokenness is hidden beneath "right" and "acceptable" Christian behavior. Performance standards have been so prioritized that woundedness has been masked, and people fear rejection if they are ever "found out." The Church in many places works at looking good, going so far in some cases as to prioritize glitter over honesty and entertainment over genuine transformation. Which of us, in such an environment, would dare share our true struggles, let alone see them as a context for Christ's ministry to others?

The record of Scripture and history testifies to a Church far more comfortable with brokenness as a context for ministry than ours is. The Bible describes believers as former adulterers, idol worshipers, prostitutes and pagans (see, for example, 1 Corinthians 6:11). It even refers to some people with reference to their brokenness: Simon the leper, the Gadarene demoniac, blind Bartimaeus. The power of their testimony was not in an acceptable personal image, but in Christ's glory. Their wounds, once touched by Jesus, were what qualified them to spread the message of hope and healing.

I believe in training and education. But in a pain-filled world, the approach of the wounded healer is the most important qualification of ministry. The effective servant is not so simply because he or she has a head full of knowledge or a wall covered with diplomas. The minister of Christ must be in touch with his or her own wounds so as to identify with the suffering of others and tell them of the eternal Wounded Healer.

For many churches, however, providing such an atmosphere of openness and vulnerability will demand great change.

An Atmosphere of Corporate Brokenness

My primary concern in writing this chapter is to encourage you to embrace the call to be a wounded healer. The response of the corporate Christian community is vital to realizing this goal. If the local church is uncomfortable with brokenness, resistant to vulnerability and continuously invested in performance, it will be difficult to embrace this model of ministry. Conversely, if a local body nurtures an atmosphere of openness, understands the value of weakness and models humility, it will be free to grow and develop in ministry as wounded healers.

I was asked to minister at a church recently that has invested heartily in performance and appearance. For more than a decade, it has expended much time and energy on image. From the professional presentation on Sunday mornings to the jacket-and-tie requirements for staff, nothing appeared out of place. Members of the pastoral staff were required to wear their hair in a certain way, to attend all meetings, to abide by clear standards of behavior and to avoid movies, certain restaurants and the like. Yes, the Gospel is preached at that church and people are being saved. But the message is not too subtle: "We reward good Christians who behave."

When I met with several members of the staff, I noticed they were one uptight group! What made matters worse was the recent dismissal of a staff member who had confessed to being in a compromising position with a member of the congregation. Certainly some restorative steps should have been taken. But the reaction of the board seemed far more punitive and panic-driven than founded on redemptive love.

As a result, the staff was more performance-bound than ever. Getting them to consider vulnerability was nigh unto impossible. Admitting struggles or wounds

239

meant only one thing: disapproval or rejection. This was one place where it was definitely not O.K. to be not O.K.

The disadvantages of this kind of closed atmosphere are many. First, the staff is not free to address their own wounds. They hide struggles behind nice haircuts and designer blazers. The heavy restraint leaves wounds festering and problems unattended, until breakdown or disqualification results. It is this kind of setting that causes a pastor struggling with impure thoughts to keep silent and stew all alone. Then, years later, he is trapped in pornography or an affair and must leave the ministry. I would rather know, wrestle with someone's problem and restore him or her lovingly while the situation is less volatile, than pretend all is well while privately seeding future disaster.

Another disadvantage is that these servants of the Lord are not able to experience the healing of Christ openly. If they were free to struggle together as a staff, confessing weakness and deep wounds, they would find the strength of Christ made real in weakness. There is a freedom that comes from such surrender that is almost indescribable. Jesus' power and presence become tangibly real. What results are new joy in Him and release from the unending, exhausting task of hiding and secretly managing the private war within. Christ becomes so powerful that, like Paul, we can delight in weakness, for then His strong presence rests upon us.

Yet another disappointment of a closed, pretentious approach to ministry is the inability to be a wounded healer. The pastoral staff of the church I visited knows how to minister through programs, principles and performance. Yet they miss the place of deepest healing to others—the flow that pours through surrendered wounds. What a tragic loss! I have experienced ministry from my strengths, but how much more effective and freeing is the ministry that flows out of brokenness. There is a quality of Christ's presence that transforms those being served. The path to such ministry obviously involves risk and pain, but the journey is well worth any price, for the wounded healer knows that his or her ministry is far more reflective of the living Christ.

Possibly most tragic is the impact that performance-based ministries have on the people. Any staff bound by appearance will keep a congregation tightly locked up. The true picture of the people is never seen, hidden behind happy smiles and "acceptable" behavior. Yet beneath the surface are wounds that fester—ground for Satan's onslaught of deception and destruction. The atmosphere encourages silence, and the unwritten no-talk rule robs countless men and women of the compassionate, noncondemning help they desperately need. It also steals every potential ministry that lies dormant in the wounds of God's people. Performance-based ministry in no way reflects the honest, open, Christ's-strength-in-weakness servanthood of the New Testament.

Changing such an approach to ministry is not easy, and initially it invites pain and a high pricetag. I know, for the impact of opening the congregation I served was tremendous. I risked rejection in sharing my own issues, trusting the Lord to sustain me through disapproval and misunderstanding. Some people left the church, uncomfortable with what was happening. Others began to address issues in their own lives left long unattended, and it was tough. But with patience and prayer and adequate preparation, we made it through to the joy of newfound freedom. Most important, God's grace was made perfect in weakness, lives were deeply changed and Jesus was singularly glorified! Ask the people of that congregation if they would ever turn back. Grace and weakness have brought the flow of Christ's healing, and now their wounds have become the context of powerful ministries.

If you want to be a wounded healer, find a community committed to grace and openness. Whether in an entire congregation or a small group, fellow pilgrims are essential to the journey. The mutual support, accountability and encouragement others bring will spur you on to growth. Compassion and acceptance will enhance healing as you feel safe enough to expose even the most hideous wound to the Lord's touch. Strengthened in the bond of unity, you can offer your own struggle as a vehicle for ministry to God's people without shame or fear of rejection. While humbling, such shared experiences draw all eyes to Jesus and every heart to deepest devotion and praise.

Comforting Others

It is likely that, since you are reading this book, you are journeying along the pathway of pain. It is a pilgrimage most of us make, often more than a few times over the span of a life. I hope that along the way you will discover many treasures within the valley of sorrow and suffering. The darkness gives up its secrets, reveals its many mysteries and jewels. Far from easy and certainly costly, the experience will enrich your life in many unexpected and needed ways.

If you are attentive, priceless possessions will become the spoils of battle. You will see God as trustworthy, find Jesus more dear and the Holy Spirit more manifestly present in life. Encountering truth is a severe mercy that frees you to let go of what was in order to lay hold of what will forever be. The journey will bring forgiveness, unlock feelings and forge relationships vital to well-being. Disciplines like prayer and praise will become open channels of grace, strengthening your faith while sending the evil one into forced retreat. Like the children of Israel in the Valley of Ber-acah, you will leave the valley of brokenness with your basket full, even if a certain amount of pain lingers or a limp persists.

But the journey is not complete until you understand that what you have received, you must give. Treasures are not for storing; they must be shared with every hurting, needy, broken person God brings your way. Every new truth, each precious insight, every blessing of comfort and hope is to be passed on in the name of Jesus Christ. Having felt the pain, you must look at the broken through new eyes and, with deep understanding and heartfelt compassion, extend whatever you have that may help. The broken will receive it with hope, for they see your wounds and scars as you give to them. Since you, the wounded healer, have been there before them, what you offer is truly priceless.

Many people think traveling into the dark night of despair disqualifies them from ministry. In the grand reversal of the Kingdom, it does just the opposite, if you allow it. It places you in the context of the broken, so as to offer healing and comfort. Paul writes:

Praise be to the God and Father of our Lord Jesus Christ, the Father of compassion and the God of all comfort, who comforts us in all our troubles, so that we can comfort those in any trouble with the comfort we ourselves have received from God. For just as the sufferings of Christ flow over into our lives, so also through Christ our comfort overflows. If we are distressed, it is for your comfort and salvation; if we are comforted, it is for your comfort, which produces in you patient endurance of the same sufferings we suffer. And our hope for you is firm, because we know that just as you share in our sufferings, so also you share in our comfort.

2 Corinthians 1:3–7

As the healing and comfort of God flow through the wounds of Christ to you, so your hurts and struggles can become a channel of hope to countless broken men, women and children. At journey's end you must be willing to extend that hand of healing, offering the treasures of darkness as the Lord's wounded healer.

Few writers have influenced me as much as the late Henri Nouwen. God gifted him to communicate profound truth in clear, simple terms. Much of what he shared was mined along his own pain-filled path. In his book *The Wounded Healer,* Nouwen told the following story.

> Rabbi Yoshua ben Levi came upon Elijah the prophet while he was standing at the entrance of Rabbi Simeron ben Yohai's cave. . . . He asked Elijah, "When will the Messiah come?" Elijah replied, "Go and ask him yourself." "Where is he?" "Sitting at the gates of the city." "How shall I know him?" "He is sitting among the poor covered with wounds. . . . He unbinds one at a time and binds it up again, saying to himself, 'Perhaps I shall be needed; if so, I must always be ready so as not to delay for a moment.'"

Nouwen goes on to comment:

> The Messiah, the story tells us, is sitting among the poor, binding his wounds one at a time, waiting for the moment when he will be needed. So it is too with the minister. . . . He must bind his own wounds carefully in anticipation of the moment when he is needed. He is called to be the wounded healer, the one who must look after his own wounds, but at the same time be prepared to heal the wounds of others.[2]

Henri Nouwen challenges you to minister with great sympathy for the human condition. This comes, as I said earlier, by facing your own woundedness and surrendering it to Christ's healing touch. Your weakness becomes the strength of Jesus, and the experience of pain the common ground you share with the lost and broken. Is this not precisely what our Lord has done for you? Has He not offered you, broken by sin, healing through His wounds? You must in turn become a channel of healing to others, admitting your woundedness while extending to all the treasure that is, by grace, yours in Christ.

Years ago a seasoned servant of the Lord told me that before God uses someone, He allows that person to be broken. He listed several examples and said that someday I, too, would walk that path, if I wanted all Christ had for me. In my immaturity and arrogance, I felt certain he was wrong. Sure, maybe others needed to walk through the fire, but I had never even considered the possibility. Then one day I realized I was in that very place, forced on a journey not of my own choosing.

Along the way I discovered that the path was well worn, for countless people had gone before me. It contained the footprints of virtually every servant of the Lord. Somewhere along the way I realized that what I had sought to avoid was a painful journey of privilege, the honored pilgrimage of a son, a path full of potential and purpose. It was then that cursing gave way slowly to blessing, and in the midst of struggling steps I began to dance.

My friend, it is not the whole and beautiful who alone can serve Christ or touch the world most effectively. It is also those wounded, broken and scarred people like you and me who have tasted of God's mercy and love and feasted on His grace and redeeming power. Frail in yourself, you can offer only His strength, for yours is now spent. Yet it is always and only His strength that is sufficient. And it takes a path such as this—the one you are possibly on now—to teach you that truth. His grace is made perfect in weakness. As such, in weakness you can rejoice.

For Further Reading:

The Wounded Healer by Henri Nouwen
Life of the Beloved by Henri Nouwen
Finding God by Larry Crabb
Healing Grace by David Seamands
Families Where Grace Is in Place by Jeff Van Vonderon

Notes

Chapter 1: God Is within the Darkness

1. The details of this season can be found in my book entitled *Wounded: How You Can Find Inner Wholeness and Healing in Him* (Camp Hill, Pa.: Christian Publications, 1994).

2. de Caussade, Jean-Pierre, *The Sacrament of the Present Moment* (San Francisco: HarperCollins, 1989), p. ix.

3. *The Cloud of Unknowing* is the title of a book on contemplative prayer written by a fourteenth-century English monk. It emphasizes finding God not through reason but through His love.

4. Our Lord Jesus modeled perfectly the proper response to suffering and pain. In Gethsemane on the night of His arrest, Christ openly embraced and expressed the spiritual and emotional upheaval in which He was caught. Weeping before the Father, Jesus struggled honestly with the darkness around Him. He met the circumstance—while painful enough to bring blood from His brow—head on. There He found more than strength and understanding. Jesus experienced union with God and peace that He was in the Father's hands. The disciples, on the other hand, chose differently. Instead of wrestling in prayer, they slept. As the darkness pressed in even more in the coming hours, they reacted and either fled, lashed out or betrayed their Lord.

5. The story of Job is the clearest example. God may not actually have caused the calamity, but He allowed it and used it for greater good.

6. See Hebrews 5:8; 12:7–11; James 1:2–4, 12; 1 Peter 1:6–9; 4:12–16.

7. de Caussade, *Sacrament*, p. 17.

8. Fénelon, François, *The Seeking Heart* (Beaumont, Tex.: Seed Sowers, 1992), pp. 11, 4.

9. Crabb, Larry, *Finding God* (Grand Rapids: Zondervan, 1993), p. 81.

10. Brother Lawrence, *The Practice of the Presence of God* (Virginia Beach, Va.: CBN University Press, 1978), p. 46.

11. Guyon, Jeanne, *Guyon Speaks Again* (Beaumont, Tex.: Seed Sowers, 1989), pp. 135–136.

Chapter 2: Life, Wholeness and Healing Flow from Jesus Christ

1. Guyon, Jeanne, *Experiencing the Depths of Jesus Christ* (Beaumont, Tex.: Seed Sowers, 1975), p. 1.

2. Edwards, Jonathan, *On Knowing Christ* (Carlisle, Pa.: Banner of Truth, 1990), p. 182.

3. Simpson, A. B., *The Christ-Life* (Camp Hill, Pa.: Christian Publications, 1980), p. 20.

4. Mulholland, Robert, *Shaped by the Word* (Nashville: Upper Room, 1985), pp. 148–149.

5. Guyon, *Depths*, p. 13.

Chapter 3: The Holy Spirit Is Always Present with You

1. Tozer, A. W., *The Counselor* (Camp Hill, Pa.: Christian Publications, 1993), p. 130.

2. I have written more extensively on these steps in *One to One: A Practical Guide to Friendship Evangelism* (Camp Hill, Pa.: Christian Publications, 1989), pp. 98–103.

Chapter 4: The Truth Will Set You Free

1. McGee, Robert S., *The Search for Significance* (Houston: Rapha Publications, 1990).

Chapter 5: Forgetting Your Past May Not Be Enough

1. A previous book I wrote, *Wounded: How You Can Find Inner Wholeness and Healing in Him*, is dedicated to the topic of inner healing. The story of Julie is also part of that volume.

Chapter 6: Feelings Tell You More Than You Think

1. Longman, Tremper III, and Dan Allender, *The Cry of the Soul* (Colorado Springs: NavPress, 1994), p. 24.

2. Ibid., pp. 26–27.

Chapter 7: Forgiveness Releases You from Torment

1. Some of the illustrations and concepts used in this chapter also appear in my previous book *Wounded: How You Can Find Inner Wholeness and Healing in Him*.

Chapter 8: Healthy Relationships Move You toward Spiritual Maturity

1. I recognize a twofold danger in using the word *spiritual* in this context. First, it can reek of pride, like the attitude of the Corinthian believers, resulting in a "we-are-better-than-you" feeling. Second, the word *spiritual* can be too broad, leading one to believe that any spiritual community is fine, even that of cults and certain sects. I address these issues more directly under the section "Find a Healthy Spiritual Community," which I hope will clarify my use of the term.

Chapter 9: Your Battle Is Not against Flesh and Blood

1. Murphy, Ed, *The Handbook for Spiritual Warfare* (Nashville: Thomas Nelson, 1992), p. 405.
2. Ibid.
3. Ibid., pp. 408–409.

Chapter 10: Praising God in the Valley Unleashes His Power

1. Prime, Derek, *Created to Praise* (Downers Grove, Ill.: InterVarsity, 1981), pp. 10–11.
2. I have included much more detail about the sacrifice of praise in my previous book *Exalt Him: Designing Dynamic Worship Services* (Camp Hill, Pa.: Christian Publications, 1988).

Chapter 11: Spiritual Disciplines Move You toward Christlikeness

1. Mulholland, Robert, *Invitation to a Journey: A Road Map for Spiritual Formation* (Downers Grove, Ill.: InterVarsity, 1993), p. 97.
2. Mulholland, *Invitation*, p. 12.
3. Ibid., p. 24.
4. de Caussade, *Sacrament*, p. 42.
5. Mulholland, *Invitation*, p. 32.
6. Ibid., pp. 36–39.
7. Nouwen, Henri, *Life of the Beloved* (New York: Crossroads, 1996).
8. Mulholland, *Invitation*, p. 47.
9. Willard, Dallas, *The Spirit of the Disciplines* (New York: Harper & Row, 1988), p. 34.
10. Willard, *Disciplines*, pp. 175–176.

Chapter 12: You Can Become a Wounded Healer

1. Crabb, Larry, *Finding God* (Grand Rapids: Zondervan, 1993), p. 11.
2. Nouwen, Henri, *The Wounded Healer* (New York: Doubleday, 1979), p. 82.

Index

Index

Index

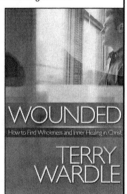

CPSIA information can be obtained
at www.ICGtesting.com
Printed in the USA
FSOW02n2139240116
16032FS